The phenomenal success of the Scarsdale Medical Diet can be explained in two words: "It works."

For more than forty years as internist, cardiologist and family doctor, Dr. Tarnower would warn patients to eat sensibly and stay trim. When they complained that diets didn't work, he decided to find a diet that *would* work.

Over twenty years ago—at the time he founded the Scarsdale Medical Center—Dr. Tarnower began developing a weight-loss program that was simple, safe—and fast. A program that made it easy to stay trim and healthy for life.

The word spread. Today the Scarsdale Diet is the salvation of millions of Americans who have never before seen such dramatic results!

The Complete Scarsdale Medical Diet

Plus
Dr. Tarnower's Lifetime Keep-Slim Program

For the first time—the TOTAL *plan for the diet that's taking America by storm, explained in full by the noted doctor who created it*

Herman Tarnower
M.D., FACP, D-IM (CV)
and
Samm Sinclair Baker

BANTAM BOOKS
TORONTO · NEW YORK · LONDON · SYDNEY · AUCKLAND

*This low-priced Bantam Book
has been completely reset in a type face
designed for easy reading, and was printed
from new plates. It contains the complete
text of the original hard-cover edition.*
NOT ONE WORD HAS BEEN OMITTED.

THE COMPLETE SCARSDALE MEDICAL DIET
A Bantam Book

PRINTING HISTORY
*Rawson Wade edition published January 1979
21 printings through October 1979
Macmillan Book Club edition April 1979
Book-of-the-Month Club edition March 1979
Preferred Choice Book Plan edition Spring 1979
Scholastic Magazine Book Club edition September 1979
Serialized in Cosmopolitan July 1979 and
Good Housekeeping Magazine April 1979.
Bantam edition / January 1980
45 printings through April 1985*

ISBN 0-553-14638-6

Published simultaneously in the United States and Canada

---

*Bantam Books are published by Bantam Books, Inc. Its trade-
mark, consisting of the words "Bantam Books" and the por-
trayal of a rooster, is Registered in U.S. Patent and Trademark
Office and in other countries. Marca Registrada. Bantam
Books, Inc., 666 Fifth Avenue, New York, New York 10103.*

PRINTED IN THE UNITED STATES OF AMERICA

H   54 53 52 51 50 49 48

Acknowledgements

We are grateful to Jean Harris for her splendid assistance in the research and writing of this book . . .

Natalie Baker organized the excellent tables, created many of the recipes, and in her quiet, intelligent way provided a great many fine suggestions . . .

Suzanne van der Vreken, an imaginative nutritionist and artist, created many of the Gourmet and International recipes . . .

We wish, especially, to thank Lynne Tryforos, Phylis Rogers, Grace Clayton, Lydia Eichhammer, and Jeevan Procter, for their assistance with the diets, writing, and manuscript preparation . . .

Also, our thanks to all the staff at the Scarsdale Medical Center for their help and patience with diet inquiries: Barbara Strauss, Linda Francis, Maria Kenny Ruth Aroldi, Terri Alesandro, Elizabeth Bennett, Phyllis Berger, Barbara Cavallo, Sandra Engstrom, Mary Fujimoto, Elaine Gracey, Margaret Gutierrez, Beth Hollender, Jean Lukaczyn, Dita Malter, Kathleen Monahan, Joan Mosca, Majda Remec, Frances Rose, Anita Schwartz, June Spinner, Victoria Spinner, Joan Tubel, William Twasutyn, Sharon Wallberg, and Florence Weitzner.

And . . . our special thanks to a brilliant gentleman and friend, Oscar Dystel, who suggested and made this book possible.

Also, high compliments to Eleanor and Kennett Rawson for their excellent editing and stewardship.

Contents

For Overseas Readers

Certain terms in this book will be unfamiliar to overseas readers. Listed below are the most important equivalents:

American	English Equivalent
Broil	Grill
Club Soda	Soda Water
Cornstarch	Cornflour
Eggplant	Aubergine
Pimiento	Red Pepper
Pot Cheese	Low calorie curd cheese
Scallion	Spring onion
Snow peas	Mange-tout peas
Squash	Marrow
Zucchini	Courgette

In addition, many American cuts of meat differ from those found in other parts of the world. Where unfamiliar cuts of steak are mentioned, we suggest you use any type of steak suitable for grilling, as long as all excess fat is cut off.

American measurements tend to be by cups, one of which is equivalent to about half an English pint. For solid food, a cup ranges between ¼ to ½ lb. depending on the density of the ingredient (i.e., a cup of rice will weigh 8 ounces compared with 4 ounces for a cup of grated cheese).

Note On Metrication

For liquid measurements, a cup is roughly equivalent to ¼ litre.

For solid ingredients, a cup will measure between 125 and 250 grammes following the same criteria as mentioned on the previous page.

For oven temperatures, please consult the list below:

	°Fahrenheit	°Celsius	Gas Mark
Cool	200	93	¼
Low	250	121	½
	275	135	1
	300	149	2
Moderate	325	163	3
	350	177	4
	375	191	5
Hot	400	205	6
	425	218	7
	445	229	8
Very Hot	470	243	9
	490	253	10
	510	265	11
	525	274	12

1
A Private Diet Goes Public...
Why the Phenomenal Success
of the Scarsdale Medical Diet

I, personally, explain the Scarsdale Medical Diet's phenomenal popularity in two words: *"It works."* A slim, trim lady said to me recently, "Your diet is beautifully simple, and the results are simply beautiful." I just say, "It works."

Any good doctor will tell you that what you eat is important to your health. Perhaps my background of over forty years as an internist, cardiologist, and family doctor has made me especially diet conscious. For all these years, I have been counseling patients to eat and drink sensibly and stay trim. I have listed for them quite specifically what they should or should not eat if they want to lose weight, or if I think they need to.

A number of years ago I decided to save time by having my diet suggestions typed up and mimeographed. If my mail has been any indication, those well-read, dog-eared, mimeographed sheets have traveled the length of this country and to many places in Europe and the Mideast.

Recently the media got the message and, suddenly sparked by newspaper and magazine articles, literally thousands of people from all over the world were calling and writing for Dr. Tarnower's "Scarsdale Medical Diet." I am told that no diet has ever been as spontaneously and unanimously acclaimed as this one. At first it took off arithmetically—one patient telling another person. As word of mouth increased, its popularity grew geometrically, nationally and internationally.

How the "Just-Right" Combination of Foods Was Created

Nobody could be more delighted and surprised at the extraordinary success of the Diet than I, since I am not a "diet doctor."

Early in my medical career, I became impressed with the importance, even the absolute necessity, of proper weight management for maximum individual health and well-being. This is especially true for the heart patient.

I would tell my overweight patients to reduce, as do so many other physicians. However, that just didn't work with most people. I would say forcefully, "You *must* take off that unhealthy fat and flab. Go on a good reducing diet immediately."

The usual reply: "I've tried all the diets I could find, and they just don't work for me, Dr. Tarnower."

I finally decided that I would have to do something about that very real problem myself. Nineteen years ago, at the time that I founded the Scarsdale Medical Center, I concentrated on creating a reducing diet that would be simple and effective. One that would keep them trim for the rest of their lives. Taking the weight off was basic, but they also had to *keep it off*—for many the most difficult aspect.

Studying other diets and their faults and flaws, I came to the conclusion that they were too complicated or too slow, overly demanding, or had other defects that turned people away.

Thus the Scarsdale Medical Diet (SMD) evolved. A great deal went into creating it, but essentially my guides were medical knowledge gained through years of medical practice, day-to-day experience with all kinds of patients, and just plain common sense.

Over the past nineteen years, patients who reduced and kept trim on the Scarsdale Medical Diet spread the news through their own improved appearance and well-being. The word got around that something phenomenal was happening in weight loss.

Teachers in some physical fitness classes distributed the Diet to hundreds of students, recommending exercise to firm off inches, and the Scarsdale Medical Diet to take off pounds.

Jogging groups took up the Diet. A nurse who lost 11 pounds quickly and easily, introduced it where she worked. Her husband, a policeman, lost 14 pounds and alerted overweight fellow officers in the New York City Police Department.

The Beach Point Club in Mamaroneck, New York, placed a sheet on its bulletin boards and dining tables announcing: "The Scarsdale Diet . . . If you're on it, Beach Point has it . . . If you're not on it, you will be . . . Every lunch in the Pavilion, every regular dinner in the dining room has a Scarsdale Diet dish on the menu." A woman on jury duty took along a Scarsdale Medical Diet lunch box, and was pleased to see others in the courtroom toting the same.

Many restaurants began to make the Scarsdale Medical Diet a menu feature.

Without my knowledge, the popularity of the diet came to the attention of a writer for *The New York Times Magazine*. In a general article on beauty, titled "Shape-Up Time," Alexandra Penney discussed the diet briefly. "A vice president of Bloomingdale's was shown the printed diet by the owner of a fish restaurant, decided to try it, lost 20 pounds in 14 days and claims he was never hungry and never tired . . ."

At about the same time, *Westchester Magazine* ran a short item on "A Diet People Are Talking About . . . 'as much as a twenty pound loss in two weeks is not unusual' . . . those who have tried it insist it's the only one that works."

The New York Times followed with an article by Georgia Dullea headlined "If it's Friday, it must be Spinach and Cheese." It reported in part, "The Scarsdale Diet: This is where the losers live, the real losers. This is the home of the famous 14-day Scarsdale diet. . . . Weight losses of up to 20 pounds in two weeks are reported here. Rarely do dieters feel hungry or cranky. . . . The Scarsdale diet is spreading. . . . Requests are coming from as far away as California and Mexico. Now London is ringing up about the Scarsdale diet. . . . Everywhere you go people are talking about the diet . . ."

A *Family Circle* magazine article stated, "Here's the diet that took the town of Scarsdale, N.Y. by storm, and now may well be sweeping the country. With it you lose up to 20 pounds in 14 days—without ever going hungry.

"This is the no-hunger, no-hassle diet that in-the-know big losers have been passing on to their friends coast-to-coast. It's the *easiest diet ever*. In exactly eight days, I had lost exactly eight pounds!

"It's an enormous relief not to have to count calories or weigh food or worry about quantities . . . you lose weight without a lot of fuss."

Sunday Woman, the new newspaper supplement magazine, in a report by Anthony Dias Blue, called it "THE ULTIMATE DIET . . . so named by a friend who had been on every diet ever invented . . . she looked relaxed, slim, crowed, 'I've been on Dr. Tarnower's Scarsdale Medical Diet, AND IT WORKED! I lost 18 pounds in 14 days, and I'm able to KEEP IT OFF!'

"The diet is tasty and filling; you can order it in any restaurant and follow it easily at home.

". . . Why the popularity of the diet? BECAUSE IT WORKS!"

Most Meaningful for YOU: Reports from Overweights

As soon as the newspaper and magazine stories appeared, thousands of letters and comments poured in from women and men who had lost weight on the Scarsdale Medical Diet. Their reports are all-important as proof for everyone, notably you, that the diet that worked wonderfully for them can work for you. Finally, there has been added demonstration and encouragement that SMD dieters not only can take off pounds and inches, but also *keep them off*.

Please realize that the enthusiastic media reports and personal "testimonials" received have been unsolicited. The people involved, aside from my patients, are primarily unknown to me. They are from about every state of the Union, including Alaska and Hawaii, and from other countries. These people are not unusual. They vary in overweight from a relatively few pounds to 50 or more.

Add to these the many formerly overweight patients who have been in my care for years. Their records prove that they *keep trim year after year* on the program that I have named the Scarsdale Lifetime Keep-Trim Program—all yours in this book.

Here are just a handful of typical comments that have come to me from thousands of dieters—some in person, from my patients, and others by mail.

"I have completed 14 days of your diet and lost 14 pounds. This is the first diet that has worked for me that isn't ridiculous starvation. It is a healthy diet that I can stick to until I reach my goal and get all my excess weight off."

(A patient): *"It's three years now* since I went on your Diet and slimmed down from 152 pounds to my desired 118 pounds. I've kept trim on your simple Two-On-Two-Off program without any trouble. As for my health, as you know from my regular checkups, most of my medical problems have disappeared. I feel better than ever. My husband keeps saying how wonderful it is to have a slim, attractive wife again, but he can hardly match my own delight about the 'new' me."

"A friend raved about how she lost weight quickly on your diet. I wasn't eager because I'm not the diet

type. I was never fat until change of life, getting older, getting heavier. I had no discipline, always good intentions that weren't good enough. I went on your diet —IT WORKED! Thank you!"

"I didn't have more than 10 pounds to lose, which I lost quickly on your diet. Results were almost immediate. I found that the daily food combinations on your menu didn't leave me hungry in the least. Best of all, I had no craving for food at night—that's always been my biggest problem. I thank you for the time and energy put into something that works and is *fun."*

(A patient): "Now that I have maintained my 165-pound weight quite steadily for over two years, it's difficult for me to believe that I was a 'fat man' who topped the scale at over 210 pounds. Since I took off the terrible load of fat and have kept it off, I breathe easily, and my vigor and endurance have been restored. I'm incredibly better at tennis and other sports. I assure you, Dr. Tarnower, with the help of your diet I'll never be a fat man again."

"I lost 14 pounds in the first two weeks on your diet, and our grown son lost 20. That's 34 pounds in our family already. You are really and truly responsible for the shedding of a lot of unwanted pounds in this area. We're absolutely delighted with the results of the diet."

Not a "Fad" Diet

Most people hear about a diet from a friend, or read about it and try it. This is not always wise. There have been more than enough fad diets, some of them actually quite dangerous to your health. But nineteen years of successful, safe weight loss by multitudes of users of the Scarsdale Medical Diet have proved beyond question that it is *not* a passing fad.

This Diet is good medical practice. A workable, proven, but rather private diet has suddenly gone public. The overwhelming response of the public and the media has encouraged me to write this book, since I not only believe the Diet can be useful to many others, but also the previously published versions of the Diet have not scratched the surface of the program's *lifetime thinning* aspects. I welcome this opportunity to share with you fully the vital, long-term dimensions of the Diet.

It is always prudent for your physician to approve and supervise your diet, and I so advise, even if you know you are in good health. Your physician knows much more about you than a stranger writing a book in Scarsdale, New York. It is my experience, however, that an otherwise healthy person, no matter how far-out his eating habits may have been, can follow the Scarsdale Medical Diet, and be reasonably comfortable with it.

At the end of fourteen days on SMD, your individual Weight Chart will tell your personal story of gratifying weight loss. I will tell you exactly how to do this charting in Chapter IV.

2
The Ingredients of the Successful Scarsdale Medical Diet

What does a diet need to be successful?

A successful diet has to start out with common sense and a little understanding of human nature. Individuals who are towers of strength will get trim on their own. You and I need some special understanding and help. A diet is useless if people can't stick to it.

A good diet must be palatable, safe, satisfying, and uncomplicated. It must show results in a reasonably short period of time. And, most important of all, it must help to develop a lifetime pattern of good eating habits so that *the weight lost will stay lost.*

As I began to develop the Scarsdale Medical Diet, these are the six basic qualities I considered most essential to success for the dieter:

1. SAFE NUTRITIONAL BALANCE

Our bodies require a combination of basic nutrients— protein, carbohydrates, fat, minerals, vitamins, and water. *You won't develop any vitamin or mineral deficiency in two weeks, even on a starvation diet,* but the Scarsdale Medical Diet happens to provide plenty of nutrients. Protein, carbohydrates, and fats are the big three nutrients, and all of them come packaged in calories—a fact we sometimes forget.

The average person's food intake contains approximately 10–15 percent protein, variations of between 40–45 percent fat and 40–50 percent carbohydrates. Fortunately we know that we can make wide variations in these percentages and still deliver a healthy diet. The Scarsdale Medical Diet averages 1,000 calories or less per day and averages 43 percent protein, 22.5

percent fat, and 34.5 percent carbohydrates. (See comparison chart at end of this chapter.)

2. RAPID WEIGHT LOSS

We are geared to a fast-moving world, and programmed to need and expect fast results. It's unrealistic to expect the average person to keep plugging along on a diet for months and months if heartening results are not soon obtained. On the Scarsdale Medical Diet, dieters may lose an average of a pound a day; many report losses of 20 or more pounds in two weeks.

Another effective, built-in support for you is that the diet is limited to fourteen days at a time. You are not discouraged by the prospect of staying on a restricted program for what seems forever. You are encouraged by the fact that in five, or nine, or fourteen days at most, *depending on how much weight you want to lose,* you'll be able to enjoy switching to a greater variety of foods on the Keep-Trim Program.

You can then have some of the additional "treats," even a cocktail, if you are so inclined. Anticipated rewards don't seem so far away when the maximum wait is fourteen days.

3. TASTY, VARIED, AND FILLING FOOD CHOICES

It is foolish to think that people will change their dietary habits over the long haul if you can't offer them reasonable options. Two weeks of nothing but bananas or cottage cheese or the like is not only boring, it is hardly the way to develop sensible, proper eating habits which will keep you at your desired weight.

Devising options that are tasty, colorful (the way food *looks* is important), and satisfying, was a large part of the Diet's challenge for me. I think as you discover the many interesting culinary options in this book you will agree that this goal has been well met.

4. SIMPLICITY AND EASE OF UNDERSTANDING AND PREPARATION

One of the most common refrains from many of my patients who have successfully followed the Diet has been, *"It's so simple!* There's no trick to staying on it." The importance of that simplicity is something I cannot overemphasize.

The more you worry about food, the more you even think about it while you're on a diet, the more difficult and tiresome the whole process can become. Here *the decisions have been made for you*, and you can get about the business of losing weight without having to ask yourself, "What shall I have for breakfast, for lunch, for dinner?"

You don't have to count calories or weigh out each portion. You don't become anxious about what you are permitted for snacks either; you munch on carrots or celery, and that's it.

Everything you eat each day is listed on that day's menus. As you will note in Chapter 4, you can, for instance, enjoy "plenty of steak," and "fruit salad, as much as you want," as long as you avoid overloading your stomach to the point of discomfort.

5. THE BEGINNING OF BEHAVIOR MODIFICATION

Any diet plan designed to tease you with swift weight loss, only to have you gain it right back again, must drive home to you the importance of changing your dietary habits for a lifetime. You will learn to eat better, eat less, develop new tastes. Pleasure and intelligent, disciplined eating need not be mutually exclusive.

You may not be consciously aware of it, and you need not be while you are on the Scarsdale Medical Diet plan, but *built-in factors* are changing your eating habits. This might be called a very simple type of "behavior modification." As one couple wrote, "We are painlessly learning good eating habits from just two weeks on the Scarsdale Medical Diet."

The process is basically *learning by doing*—no stress, no strain, no complicated study or other confusion. You follow the simple eating instructions precisely. You are not put off or confused by a bewildering array of choices. You enjoy eating what is listed for you each day, and you will find it easier than you anticipated to avoid high-carbohydrate, high-calorie food.

Following the Scarsdale Medical Diet *exactly as written* is a discipline that can be the beginning of good dietary habits that will keep you trim through your lifetime.

6. THE DIET HAD TO BE PRACTICAL FOR EATING OUT IN A RESTAURANT OR ELSEWHERE

One patient told me, "After a week on your diet, I went off to a resort hotel for our vacation. I had no trouble being served the food I required, and I continued to lose weight happily."

What Does Your Body Need to Stay Healthy?

The body is the product of what it eats. The most obvious and probably the most common nutritional defects are caused by serious calorie *imbalance:* too few calories or too many. Chronic food shortages are the cause of much of the world's malnutrition. But remember that the word "malnutrition" means not only inadequate intake or assimilation of food but an *unbalanced* intake or assimilation as well.

You can be malnourished in affluent suburbia as well as in the Third World. In most cases, it often takes the form of eating too much of the wrong things.

As a cardiologist, I can assure you that being *overweight* is an important contributing factor in cardiovascular diseases. Consequently, *weight loss* is an important contributing factor in cardiovascular disease *prevention*. Excess fat can have a seriously deleterious effect on your blood pressure and blood cholesterol.

As an internist, I know that while it isn't the basic cause of diabetes, osteoarthritis, or gall bladder diseases, excess weight can aggravate all three of these diseases, and many others, also, to a serious degree.

A study in progress, under the auspices of the Navy's Center for Prisoner of War Studies in San Diego, suggests that the low-cholesterol low-fat diet of Navy pilots imprisoned during the Vietnam War contributed to their long-term physical health!

A control group of other Navy pilots, matched with returned prisoners by such variables as age, marital status, rank, schooling, and so forth, showed a higher incidence of cardiovascular disease. In general, they were less healthy than their P.O.W. counterparts. No liquor, reduced rations, and foods undoubtedly lower in cholesterol and fat than the average American diet are listed as important contributing factors to these results. I hasten to add—this is hardly my formula for losing weight! But there is a message in it.

How Much Should You Weigh?

Take a moment to look over the chart that follows. We will discuss it more fully after you have examined it.

DESIRED WEIGHT CHART
(Based on height; no clothing.)

HEIGHT	WOMEN (weight in pounds)	MEN (weight in pounds)
4'10"	90–98	95–105
4'11"	93–102	98–108
5'	95–105	100–111

DESIRED WEIGHT CHART
(Based on height; no clothing.)

HEIGHT	WOMEN (weight in pounds)	MEN (weight in pounds)
5'1"	97–108	105–117
5'2"	100–111	110–123
5'3"	105–118	115–128
5'4"	110–123	120–133
5'5"	112–126	125–138
5'6"	117–130	130–143
5'7"	120–134	133–148
5'8"	125–139	137–153
5'9"	130–144	143–159
5'10"	135–149	148–164
5'11"	140–154	152–168
6'	144–158	155–171
6'1"		163–179
6'2"		167–183
6'3"		170–188
6'4"		172–195
6'5"		178–198
6'6"		185–206

The chart shows recommended weights arrived at through medical experience and prolonged study by life insurance companies of long-lived people. The figures are not offered as "ideal" or "perfect" weights, but statistics show there is wisdom and guidance in them for those who wish to live a long, healthy life.

If you consume more calories (units of energy) than your age, size, and life style require, you store those calories in the form of fat. If you consume fewer calories than you need, you lose fat—because the body uses fat as an energy source when it runs out of calories.

Since we must take into account many variables—such as age, sex, bone structure, climate, profession—in our individual caloric needs, you won't necessarily fit any chart exactly, but must look at the figures in relation to your own situation.

It is very well for some nutritionists to say that dieting is too personal, too different, for each person to follow the same popular diet. Of course, it is doubly important when an illness is involved, or someone is seriously obese; a doctor must then tailor a diet to the individual. But the fact is, the vast majority of overweight people will never have a diet designed just for each one, with every personal variable noted and catered to.

A certain number of calories are needed to sustain the basic body metabolism, which includes such functions as keeping the heart beating, breathing, and maintaining a normal body temperature. Beyond that, each of your activities requires calories. If sitting is as active as you get, your calorie need is small. If long-distance swimming is your thing, the calorie needs are quite different.

If sitting is your "activity," I recommend that you mend your ways quickly! Always remember that a trim, healthy body is the product of a *total life style* that combines both the right kind of eating and activity.

In judging your own desired weight, if there should be a wide discrepancy between what you think and what your doctor thinks is your best weight, *it's the better part of wisdom to listen to him.* Obesity can sneak up on you so slowly that you don't notice it, or you've already grown used to it. Yet nothing is more menacing to your health. Weigh yourself every morning on arising.

What Nutrients Does the Body Need to be Well Nourished?

I have chosen to list nutritional needs for you in the clearest, most basic terms. Long and valuable books about nutrition have already been written, and new ones are in process as nutritional detectives uncover more of the chemical mysteries of our bodies. For the purposes of this book, it is enough for you to be familiar with what nutrients are essential to you, what services they perform for you, and what foods in the Scarsdale Medical Diet contain these necessary elements:

PROTEINS
Proteins provide the amino acids necessary to produce enzymes, antibodies, and cells for growth, maintenance and repair of tissues. Enzymes are needed to regulate body processes. Antibodies fight infection and disease.

Proteins are found in the Scarsdale Medical Diet in fish, meat, poultry, protein bread, cheese.

CARBOHYDRATES
Carbohydrates are primarily an energy source. The body will burn carbohydrates in preference to proteins and thus "spare" or conserve proteins so they can fulfill their primary function of tissue replacement. Complex carbohydrates, such as fruits, vegetables, and whole grains, also provide bulk for proper elimination. (Complex carbohydrates are *not* the same as the simple carbohydrates in sugar and starches.)

Carbohydrates are found in the Scarsdale Medical Diet in the protein bread, fruits, and vegetables allowed you.

FATS

Fats provide a concentrated source of energy. They furnish protection for various vital organs, and body insulation. Fat is especially helpful in making food palatable, but consumption of fats in excess is sure to result in weight problems.

Fats are found in the Scarsdale Medical Diet in meat, eggs, cheese, poultry, and nuts.

VITAMINS AND MINERALS

The vitamins and minerals we all need daily are found in the Scarsdale Medical Diet as follows:

Vitamin A—leafy vegetables, cheese, eggs
Vitamin D—fish
Vitamin E—leafy vegetables, nuts, eggs
Vitamin K—green vegetables
Vitamin C—fruits and vegetables—especially all that grapefruit

B VITAMINS

Vitamin B_1—grain, meats, poultry, fish, legumes
Vitamin B_2—cheese, eggs, meats, leafy vegetables
Niacin—poultry, meats, fish, leafy vegetables
Pyridoxine (B_6)—meats
Pantothenic Acid—meats, fish, eggs, vegetables
Vitamin B_{12}—meats, fish, eggs, cheese
Folic Acid—meats, fruits, eggs
Biotin—meats, eggs, legumes, nuts

Iron—meats, poultry, shellfish, eggs, nuts, green leafy vegetables, fruits
Calcium—cheese, cottage cheese, salmon, shellfish, broccoli

Phosphorus—meats, poultry, fish, cheese, nuts
Iodine—shellfish, saltwater fish
Copper—meats, shellfish, nuts
Magnesium—meats, nuts
Potassium—fruits, vegetables, meats, fish
Zinc—green leafy vegetables, fruits, meats, vegetables

Protein-Fat-Carbohydrates Composition of the Scarsdale Medical Diet

The charts below show the following:
PROTEIN intake is more than tripled—up from 10–15 percent to 43 percent—compared with the typical American diet.*
FAT consumption has been cut almost in half—down from 40–45 percent to 22.5 percent.
CARBOHYDRATE consumption has been cut considerably—down from 40–50 percent to 34.5 percent.

This a carefully planned, effective balance of Protein-Fat-Carbohydrates (P-F-C) on the Scarsdale Medical Diet. The balance changes when you shift to a greater variety of foods on Keep-Trim Eating.

To speed the reducing process, I have cut the fat consumption way down during the Diet period. When the body demands more fat, *it pulls it out of the fat storage areas, which are plentiful in the overweight woman and man.*

If you are overweight, I urge you to go on the very low-fat Scarsdale Medical Diet now (with your doctor's approval and continuing supervision), and then continue on Keep-Trim Eating and the Scarsdale Medical Diet plan for lifetime benefits.

---

* Harrison's *Principles of Internal Medicine,* 8th ed. (New York: McGraw-Hill, 1977), p. 438.

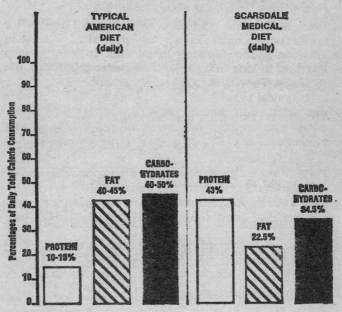

PERCENTAGES OF CALORIES CONSUMED
IN PROTEIN–FAT–CARBOHYDRATES

3
The Mystery of Diet Chemistry

Perhaps it is the reaction of many to the mania for "junk foods," but I find a great renewal of interest in nutrition and food among my patients. It is not enough for them to look trimmer and feel better than they have for years. They want to know *how* it happened.

A typical patient said to me recently, "I know your diet works. I took off 18 pounds in 14 days, and I feel great. But *how* does it work? And why does it seem much less tedious to follow than other diets I've tried?"

Part of this interest springs from a healthy curiosity about our bodies, as well as from the intense desire to lose weight. A simplified explanation may be helpful.

Metabolism and Ketones Play a Major Role

The highly sophisticated processes by which our foods are metabolized by the body are still not fully understood, even by scientists. In lay terms, however, a basic outline of the process will be of interest to serious dieters.

No one can produce reducing "miracles" through chemical wizardry. *But* a carefully designed combination of foods can increase the fat-burning process in the human system, and this means weight loss. The SMD provides such a combination of foods and, with the increased metabolism of fats, makes it possible to lose an average of a pound or more each day.

Two words, *metabolism* and *ketones* are central to weight loss in a good diet.

Sometimes, especially under proper dieting conditions, the body gets ahead of itself by burning up more fat than it does ordinarily. When this happens, your body produces an excess of *ketones*.

Ketones are sometimes referred to as the products of partially burned (or metabolized) fat. If you are not taking in enough carbohydrates or fats to supply your caloric needs, your system first draws upon your stored body fat to supply your energy needs. But your body does not succeed in completely consuming all the fat it attempts to metabolize in your cells. The waste product of this process—the partially burned fat, or "ashes" —are called ketones. If you are producing them, it is a sign that your body is burning off fat at an accelerated rate; you are enjoying *Fast Fat Metabolism*. And that is what we want—the utilization of fat stores for calories and energy. Pulling excess fat out of the fat storage areas is an integral part of an effective reducing process; your body becomes a fat-burning machine.

One of the best things about ketones for the would-be weight loser is that they act to *curb the appetite,* thus making the whole dieting process less burdensome and cutting down any need you might feel for appetite-depressing drugs. Ketones are washed out of the system through the urine. This diuretic effect is a helpful, cleansing part of the increased fat-burning process.

The foods allowed on the SMD provide what has proved to be an effective combination of proteins, fats, and carbohydrates. The combination of foods you eat daily on the Diet causes increased body fat metabolism and the production of ketones, *but not at more than a desirable level* for the average adult in normal health.

The reducing diet causing ketosis never rises to levels that might be dangerous except in the following conditions: severe, uncontrolled diabetes; third trimester pregnancy; alcoholism (the problem in the alcoholic is complicated and not fully understood).

In alcoholism, ketosis is readily reversed with glucose or insulin. In any case, as I caution repeatedly, those who have serious medical disorders, particularly alcoholism and diabetes, should diet *only under a personal physician's supervision.*

4
The Complete
Scarsdale Medical Diet

The purpose of this book is to share with others what I have shared with patients for many years—some common-sense talk about food, and some uncomplicated, proven diets for those of you who want to lose weight.

Keep this in mind always: *The SMD plan works, when you work with it*. If you think you are following the diet accurately, but aren't losing weight, double-check the instructions. No matter how many times in the past you have failed to reduce, this plan should work for you swiftly, pleasantly, and lastingly.

Normally, you will be able to lose an average of a pound a day on the Diet, and as much as 20 pounds or more in two weeks. This has been true for patients from teenagers to septuagenarians. *And more than 90 percent of those patients, once trimmed down, have maintained their desired weight*.

To begin with, let's examine the program:

1. THE SCARSDALE MEDICAL DIET (SMD)
This is a basic weight loss plan for adults who have no special dietary needs or problems. However, you will find in this book many variations of the basic Diet that have been devised to meet particular needs and responses to reasonable suggestions, here told to you for the first time.

The question arose, "Your diet is great for people who can buy lamb chops and steak. How about other people?" The Money-Saver Diet was born.

"What do I do if I have guests?" The Gourmet Diet took shape. Similarly, the Vegetarian Diet and International Diet were born.

"Why does it always have to be grapefruit for breakfast? Grapefruit isn't very good in midsummer, and other fresh fruits are at their peak then." Seasonal suggestions were added.

In short, what you will find here are diets that fill people's needs. They are designed to make sense to people, and to *work*.

2. THE KEEP-TRIM PROGRAM (KTP)

You should not remain on the basic SMD for more than two weeks at a time. Chances are you could remain on it longer without any ill effects, but I recommend that you switch at the end of two weeks to the Keep-Trim Program. This offers you a greatly expanded list of foods to choose from, and even permits a cocktail if you wish. Most dieters continue to lose a few more pounds under this program.

If, at the end of two weeks on the Keep-Trim Program, you need to lose more pounds, return for two more weeks to SMD. Under this unique Two-On–Two-Off program, you continue to lose weight safely and sensibly until you reach your desired weight.

The rapid loss weeks are spelled by periods of slower loss.

Why Will You Succeed Now Regardless of Past Failures

The unique, exclusive advantages of the Two-On–Two-Off combination plan, and its original elements, make all the difference between past failure and future success for many.

During the first two weeks on the Scarsdale Medical Diet, you will be delighted and *encouraged* by rapid weight loss, actually seeing on the scale that pounds are dropping off day by day (not that discouraging pound or two a week).

Furthermore, although you are losing weight without hunger, feeling better and enjoying increased energy and vigor, you look forward to more food freedom at the end of the fourteen days.

Looking ahead to a reward, in essence, is a vital part of the plan's successful results. From the viewpoint of your *good health,* changing your eating patterns for these two-week periods avoids troubles that might possibly arise from sustained weight loss. I will take no chances with your health.

When you have reached the healthy, slim, trim weight you want to achieve, you will have begun to develop the good eating habits that can keep you trim for a lifetime. Following the general Keep-Trim Program, you can be your own guide and enjoy the foods and beverages of your choice within the sensible guidelines set up. Of course, you will have to observe moderation always.

One of my patients said to me recently about the Scarsdale Two-On–Two-Off combination, "Dr. Tarnower, this is the ultimate lifetime program. I may have other problems one of these days, but overweight is never again going to be one of them."

3. THE FOUR-POUND STOP SIGNAL

There is no more useful ritual to add to your personal health program than a daily weighing-in. For cardiac patients it is essential; for the rest of us it is extremely helpful. Weigh yourself, "a la mode," every morning; if you do it with clothes on, you begin to kid yourself that the extra pound and a half is really your shirt or blouse. Any time that your scale hits *four* pounds over your desired weight, reach for SMD—quickly. Stay on it until the four pounds are gone. It shouldn't take a week.

Vacation times are probably the hardest time to diet, and perhaps the least appropriate. Who knows when you'll have another opportunity to sample that Bouillabaisse in Marseilles, or kidney pie in Belfast, or the

Lobster à la Nage in Brussels, or Quenelle de brochet at Lameloise in Chagny, France; I could go on and on.

Good food is one of life's great arts and great pleasures and shouldn't be by-passed even by dieters. I must confess though, that even in the heart of Kenya, or Bahrein, or Bulgaria, I've been known to weigh myself on baggage scales and then try to transpose from kilos to pounds to give myself the bad news. Tips on what to do after you've enjoyed a good vacation will be found later in the book.

4. YOUR DAILY WEIGHT CHART

This is the very personal part of the diet program for you. Set yourself a final goal for your weight loss. *What do you think your ideal weight should be?* Check the "Desired Weight Chart" in Chapter 2. At what weight do you look and feel best? Make a simple chart like the one that follows, and keep it daily. It's a good idea to keep it well beyond the two-week Diet period, too.

You can start any day of the week, using the printed menu for that day. Whether you begin on Monday or Wednesday, or any other day—that's your "Day 1" for being on the diet. If you start on a Friday, for example, you conclude your fourteen days on a Thursday. Then you switch to Keep-Trim Eating.

How to Chart Your Daily Weight

You weigh yourself first thing every morning on the Scarsdale Medical Diet to check your progress toward your desired goal. Here are some typical weight charts of SMD dieters:

Ms. W.R.—age 26, 5'5"—desired weight, 120 pounds

	DAY 1	DAY 2	DAY 3	DAY 4	DAY 5	DAY 6	DAY 7
FIRST WEEK	146	144	143	142	140	139	138
SECOND WEEK	137	136	134	133	132	131	130

TOOK OFF 16 POUNDS

Mr. E.G.—age 42, 5'10"—desired weight, 155 pounds

	DAY 1	DAY 2	DAY 3	DAY 4	DAY 5	DAY 6	DAY 7
FIRST WEEK	204	203	201	199	197	195	194
SECOND WEEK	193	191	190	188	186	185	183

TOOK OFF 21 POUNDS

Note this typical chart of a woman who started on a Tuesday instead of Monday. On Day 1 on the chart, she ate from the specified Tuesday menu, but wrote down her weight as Day 1, and proceeded naturally from there:

Mrs. P.L.—age 37, 5'4"—desired weight, 118 pounds

	DAY 1	DAY 2	DAY 3	DAY 4	DAY 5	DAY 6	DAY 7
FIRST WEEK	152	151	150	149	149	148	147
SECOND WEEK	145	144	142	141	139	139	138

TOOK OFF 14 POUNDS

You will find that filling in the daily chart is another helpful part of the answers to "How does it work?" A dieter told me, "Marking my morning weight on the chart turned out to be fun. It became like a game, recording proof positive that I was making progress. I saw my weight decreasing almost every day, some days more than others. Eventually, though, the distance between my waist and the waistband on my skirts was even better to watch than the chart. I'm on Keep-

Trim Eating now and it works. I haven't gained back what I lost."

A vital reminder to anyone who is about to go on any diet: It is important to have your physician approve and supervise the recommended menus and check your progress. Your doctor knows more about *you* than a stranger who is writing a book, as I've mentioned.

Now—off with that excess weight. Here's the Diet—to your good health!

Scarsdale Diets Basic Rules

The basic rules are simple. Refer to them whenever you are in doubt.

1. Eat exactly what is assigned. Don't substitute.
2. Don't drink any alcoholic beverages.
3. Between meals you eat only carrots and celery, but you may have as much as you wish.
4. The only beverages allowed are regular or decaffeinated coffee, black; tea; club soda (with lemon, if desired); and diet sodas in all flavors. You may drink as often as you wish.
5. Prepare all salads without oil, mayonnaise, or other rich dressings. Use only lemon and vinegar, or the vinaigrette or mustard dressing in Chapter 8, or dressings in Chapter 10.
6. Eat vegetables without butter, margarine, or other fat; lemon may be used.
7. All meat should be very lean; remove all visible fat before eating. Remove skin and fat from chicken and turkey before eating.
8. It is not necessary to eat everything listed, but don't substitute or add. Indicated combinations should be observed.

9. Never overload your stomach. When you feel full,
   STOP!
10. Don't stay on the Diet more than fourteen days.

**KEEP THIS 14-DAY PROGRESS CHART OF YOUR
WEIGHT LOSS:**

	DAY 1	DAY 2	DAY 3	DAY 4	DAY 5	DAY 6	DAY 7
FIRST WEEK							
SECOND WEEK							

TOOK OFF ___ POUNDS

The Scarsdale Medical 14-Day Diet

BREAKFAST EVERY DAY:

½ grapefruit—if not available, use fruits in
season
1 slice of protein bread, toasted, no spread
added
Coffee/tea (no sugar, cream or milk)

MONDAY

Lunch:

Assorted cold cuts (your choice—lean meats,
chicken, turkey, tongue, lean beef—see list)
Tomatoes—sliced, broiled, or stewed
Coffee/tea/diet soda

Dinner:

Fish or shellfish, any kind
Combination salad, as many greens and vege-
tables as you wish
1 slice of protein bread toasted
Grapefruit—if not available, use fruits in season
Coffee/tea

TUESDAY

Lunch:

Fruit salad, any combination of fruits, as much as you want

Coffee/tea

Dinner:

Plenty of broiled, lean hamburger

Tomatoes, lettuce, celery, olives, Brussels sprouts, or cucumbers

Coffee/tea

WEDNESDAY

Lunch:

Tuna fish or salmon salad (oil drained off), with lemon and vinegar dressing

Grapefruit, or melon, or fruit in season

Coffee/tea

Dinner:

Sliced roast lamb, all visible fat removed

Salad of lettuce, tomatoes, cucumbers, celery

Coffee/tea

THURSDAY

Lunch:

Two eggs, any style (no fat used in cooking)

Low-fat cottage cheese

Zucchini, or string beans, or sliced or stewed tomatoes

1 slice of protein bread, toasted

Coffee/tea

Dinner:

       Roast, broiled, or barbecued chicken, all you
          want—(skin and visible fat removed before
          eating)

       Plenty of spinach, green peppers, string beans

       Coffee/tea

FRIDAY

Lunch:

       Assorted cheese slices

       Spinach, all you want

       1 slice of protein bread, toasted

       Coffee/tea

Dinner:

       Fish or shellfish

       Combination salad, any and as much fresh
          vegetables as desired, including cold, diced
          cooked vegetables, if you prefer

       1 slice of protein bread, toasted

       Coffee/tea

SATURDAY

Lunch:

       Fruit salad, as much as you want

       Coffee/tea

Dinner:

       Roast turkey or chicken

       Salad of tomatoes and lettuce

       Grapefruit or fruit in season

       Coffee/tea

SUNDAY

Lunch:

Cold or hot turkey or chicken

Tomatoes, carrots, cooked cabbage, broccoli, or cauliflower

Grapefruit, or fruit in season

Coffee/tea

Dinner:

Plenty of broiled steak, all visible fat removed before eating; any cut of steak you wish—sirloin, porterhouse, London broil, etc.

Salad of lettuce, cucumbers, celery, tomatoes (sliced or cooked)

Brussels sprouts

Coffee/tea

SCARSDALE MEDICAL DIET—SUBSTITUTE LUNCH:

If you wish, you may substitute the following lunch for any lunch, any day, on the Scarsdale Medical Diet.

½ cup low-fat pot cheese or cottage cheese, mixed with 1 tablespoon of low-fat sour cream

Sliced fruit, all you want

6 halves of walnuts or pecans, whole or chopped, and mixed with the above or sprinkled over the fruit

Coffee/tea/no-sugar diet soda of any flavor

SECOND WEEK OF SCARSDALE MEDICAL DIET

Repeat all menus of the first week. It's as simple as that. If after fourteen days, you still need to lose more weight, switch to Keep-Trim Eating for two weeks, as instructed in Chapter 6.

5
Answers to Your Questions on Beginning the Scarsdale Medical Diet

The Diet looks simple and *is* simple, but still questions do arise in the mind of the dieter. Here are questions frequently asked me. Perhaps the answers will prove useful to you, too.

Q. *I want to lose five pounds. How long should I stay on the Diet?*

A. This will vary for different people. Remember that the average weight loss on SMD is one pound per day. You should certainly accomplish your goal in less than the two-week period. Always keep KTP (Keep-Trim Program) in mind for a slower loss, and "cheat" only when you know you can afford it.

Q. *Can I shift the lunch menu to dinner, and dinner to lunch, etc?*

A. Once you begin to make changes, the chink in the wall is there, and the next chink is a little easier to make. Switch only if circumstances and common sense dictate it. And perhaps I should add, "good manners," as well. I was told about a woman who insisted that her hostess defrost a steak for her "because Sunday dinner on my Scarsdale Diet says plenty of broiled steak." I hope she wasn't one of my patients.

Q. *Since the diet promotes the production of ke-tones, is it necessary to drink a great deal of water in order to help wash out the increased amount of ketones through the urine?*

A. Drinking a lot of water is usually a good habit. However, on the Scarsdale Medical Diet, take fluids as desired—*as your own body dictates.* The *moderately*

31

increased ketone production does not require drinking a specified quantity of water or other liquids.

Q. *Is this Diet safe for everyone?*

A. All the Scarsdale Medical Diets are designed to reduce adult women and men in normal health; all individuals, especially those with medical problems, and pregnant women, should not go on this or any other diet without the full approval of their personal physician.

Q. *When you list* steak *on the menu, should that be a particular type of steak, such as sirloin?*

A. Any type of *lean* steak is fine—sirloin, porterhouse, filet, London broil. And the truth is that your lower-cost cuts are even better from a dieting standpoint, because they aren't as "marbleized" with fat. Round steak, chuck, even a good old-fashioned pot roast will do very well. Proper marinating can make the less-expensive cuts very palatable. Chapter 9 has recipes for excellent marinades. Just remember that *all* visible fat must be trimmed off. (When you eat leftover steak or other meats, such as "cold cuts," you will usually find additional fat to trim.)

Q. *Should tomatoes always be eaten plain sliced, or can they be broiled or stewed?*

A. You may serve tomatoes and other vegetables, like carrots or celery, any way you choose, raw or cooked, as long as they are not prepared with fats. For instance, you will find an excellent, simple recipe for Broiled Tomato Supreme on the Gourmet Diet in Chapter 8. You may use this any time that tomatoes appear on any of the Scarsdale Diets. Fresh tomatoes may be seasoned with salt and herbs.

Q. *Are no substitutes whatsoever permitted on the Diet? Suppose I can't get one of the foods listed?*

A. In one form or another, this is probably the most frequently repeated question. While it may seem like splitting hairs to some, I think it is important to *follow the diet as written.* Your *attitude* toward a diet is an important ingredient in the success or failure of that diet for you. When you start playing fast and loose with it, you're on your way off the Diet.

Of course, as I have said elsewhere in this book, common sense is also an important ingredient in the SMD. If, for some reason, you are stymied and can't get the spinach or zucchini that is called for that day, then obviously the sensible thing to do is to substitute a similar food from another day. In the same way, your "assorted cold cuts" could be entirely sliced beef, if cold beef is what you have in the refrigerator—or cold lamb, or turkey, or chicken, or any combination of them with any fat cut off.

One important piece of advice may help you here. Plan ahead before you start the Diet. Shop for it. Have the right foods on hand and *then* begin the Diet. Dieting is serious business, even though it can be an enjoyable challenge and ultimately prove very satisfying. Don't start to diet on an impulse. Think about it; know that you're ready to make a commitment; buy what you need for it (and contrariwise, get the whipped cream, butter, and booze out of sight); and then settle in to lost weight.

Q. *I'm allergic to grapefruit, and I hate zucchini. Do I have to eat it if I don't like it?*

A. Same old question again in a slightly different guise. If you're allergic to grapefruit or anything else on the Diet, of course you don't eat it. As for "not liking" what is on the Diet, that's something else again. Obviously, you aren't going to stay on a diet long enough to profit from it, if you "gag" every time you think about zucchini or green pepper, or whatever. By the same token, remember that part of the purpose of this Diet and, certainly an important aspect of its ultimate value to you, is that it should help you to *change your eating habits.* If you're going to give up some of those "golden oldies," you're going to have to be developing enjoyment in new tastes. Teach yourself to like some of these foods, if you don't already. Raw carrots, celery, green pepper, zucchini should be the snack food in your refrigerator for the whole family, not just for the dieters. Children should find them readily available, when they reach for a snack, instead of the ubiquitous, sugar-coated "stuff" that helps buy yachts for dentists. But that's another subject.

Q. *I'm not familiar with protein bread—what is it?*

A. This description, printed by the Toronto, Canada, *Globe and Mail,* is excellent: "Protein bread is simply bread with an enriched protein content. All bread must be rated according to a calculation based on both the amount and the quality of protein it contains—a rating of 20 or higher means the bread is a good source of protein; 40 or higher, an excellent source . . . X-Brand Protein Bread (many brands are available, according to locality) contains soya concentrate and has a protein rating of 27.9, compared to 12.6 for ordinary X-Brand white bread."

Protein bread has a delicious, nutty flavor, and tastes especially good toasted. I suggest that you munch it in very small bites to fully enjoy it.

Q. *I have difficulty finding protein bread at the store here in the deep country; can I substitute any other type of bread?*

A. If protein bread is not available, you may substitute whole wheat bread (as dense as possible), or gluten bread.

Q. *What is low-fat pot cheese?*

A. Low-fat pot cheese is similar to low-fat cottage cheese. Either one or the other will do where listed on the Scarsdale Medical Diets menus.

Q. *Are Italian espresso coffee, dark French roast, and other types of coffee permitted on the Scarsdale Medical Diet?*

A. Yes, you may enjoy any type of coffee at any time—always without sugar, cream, or milk added; sugar substitute may be used. Don't drink any instant coffee which is prepared with sugar, powdered milk, or cream. (Check the ingredients on the packages.)

Q. *Is decaffeinated coffee better on the Diet than regular coffee?*
A. Either may be used—it's a matter of personal choice. If caffeine doesn't agree with you, drink decaffeinated coffee, of course.

Q. *I like plain club soda with a slice of lemon or lime—is that permitted on the Diet?*
A. Yes, it's an excellent thirst-quenching drink.

Q. *Can I have all the no-sugar diet soda I want every day?*
A. Yes, in whatever variety of flavors you like. Of course, don't drown yourself in diet sodas. You may substitute diet sodas for coffee or tea at any meal. They make a refreshing in-between meal drink, as well.

Q. *I like raw cauliflower, radishes, cucumber, and turnip slices; can I snack on them, as well as on raw carrots and celery which are listed on the Diet menus?*
A. For the first two weeks on the basic Scarsdale Medical Diet, stick to the Diet as listed. After two weeks on Keep-Trim Eating, if you go back on one of the Scarsdale Diets to lose more weight, you can add the foods you mention.

Q. *On the "substitute," can I have six whole walnuts or pecans, or only six halves, the way they're usually packed?*
A. You will find that six halves are more than enough; another half or two won't make that much difference.

Q. *Is it better to choose "low-fat pot cheese," rather than "low-fat cottage cheese" where I'm given a choice on the Diet? Also, can I substitute "farmer cheese" for either of the others?*

A. Either low-fat pot cheese or low-fat cottage cheese may be used; both are excellent. "Farmer cheese" is not permitted on the diet; it contains too much fat.

Q. *If I start the Scarsdale Medical Diet on Monday, and eat a rich dinner on Saturday, does that ruin the whole week's benefits?*

A. It doesn't "ruin" the effectiveness of the Diet, but it is damaging and can slow up your weight loss considerably.

Q. *If I eat less on a Monday than specified on the Diet listing, can I add to Tuesday's menu what I left out on Monday?*

A. It's best not to increase any day's eating. Your aim is to lose weight, not play games. Eat only as much as you want at each meal.

Q. *Do you advise any special exercise or activity while I'm on the Diet?*

A. I recommend, if at all possible, that you walk briskly at least two miles a day. If you enjoy swimming, golf, tennis, and other sports, go to it. You'll find more about this elsewhere in the book.

Q. *Why do I have to stop the Diet after two weeks? Would it be bad for me to keep going on the Diet?*

A. The entire Scarsdale dieting program is carefully planned for the most effective weight loss. This is explained in detail elsewhere in the book. Follow instructions; work with the Diet plan as specified, and it will work for you.

Q. *I'm afraid that I won't be getting enough fat and carbohydrates on the diet; isn't that so?*

A. The Scarsdale Medical Diet is LOW fat, LOW carbohydrates, and consequently LOW in caloric content, not NO fat, NO carbohydrates. The person in normal health gets enough "complex carbohydrates" in the vegetables and fruits on the diet for safe eating. He burns his own excess fat to provide the added energy needed while reducing.

Q. *What if I find myself not feeling well while I'm on the Diet—what should I do?*
A. The Diet is planned carefully to provide what is needed. Thousands of dieters have reported successful weight reduction on the SMD; most of them describe how much better it has made them feel. However, if you don't feel well at any point, *STOP*. Go to Keep-Trim Eating for a day or two, then return to the SMD. Start again with Day 1. If you continue to feel poorly, stop at once, and see your physician.

There is nothing about the combination of simple, nutritious foods on the Diets that should disagree with the healthy individual. Food allergies are always a possibility. No physician can predict who can, or cannot, eat strawberries, lobster, and so forth.

Q. *I enjoy drinking "spiced tea" and exotic teas from all over the world—Darjeeling, Jasmine, and others—are all the teas permitted on the Diet?*
A. Yes, have the tea of your choice, served hot or iced. You may add a lemon slice, cinnamon stick, or spices, as desired. Don't use any instant teas that have sugar added; those sweetened by a sugar substitute are fine.

Q. *May I drink herb teas on the Diet, such as peppermint, wintergreen, sassafras, and others?*
A. Yes, as long as they are not prepared with any kind of sugar, honey, or other caloric sweeteners.

Q. *Is there any special kind of grapefruit you recommend for the Scarsdale Medical Diet?*

A. Any tasty grapefruit is fine. There is no "magic" in any one variety, despite a sign displayed by a supermarket, "THIS grapefruit for the Scarsdale Medical Diet."

Q. *Must I drink coffee or tea on the Diet? I don't usually drink them.*
A. No, drink plain water, club soda, no-sugar diet sodas of any flavor.

Q. *When you specify olives, do you mean green, or black, or any other type, and how many at a meal?*
A. Where olives are specified on the menu, you may have *four* at the meal—green, black, Greek, Italian, whichever you prefer.

Q. *Should spinach, where listed on the Diet Menus, always be eaten raw?*
A. No, you may eat the spinach raw or cooked, seasoned to your taste, but use no fats in preparation; the same applies to other vegetables permitted. I personally like a squeeze of lemon on spinach.

Q. *Just eating a slice of protein bread at a time, how can I keep the loaf fresh-tasting?*
A. Keep the protein bread in the freezer, and take out and toast a slice at a time. It will keep fresh-tasting. The same is true for gluten, whole wheat, and practically any kind of bread.

Q. *If I can't get good fresh grapefruit in the stores, can I eat canned grapefruit, or grapefruit juice instead?*
A. If fresh grapefruit, cantaloupe, other melons, or fruits in season are not available, you may use *unsweetened*, canned grapefruit juice or slices. However, I prefer that you eat whole grapefruit or other fruits which provide bulk, and are more satisfying.

Q. *In making fruit salad, must the fruits all be fresh, or can I use canned and frozen fruits?*

A. When fruits are specified on the menu, they should preferably be fresh. Canned or frozen may be used, as long as they are *not* packed with sugar, or any other caloric sweetener. Sugar substitutes are permitted.

Q. *Can I really have any kind of shellfish where you list "fish" on the menu, as on Friday's dinner?*

A. Yes, you may enjoy shrimps, lobster, scallops, crab, oysters, clams, mussels, and so on. None of the fish or shellfish dishes should be prepared or served with any fats, oils, butter, or margarine. Cocktail sauce may be used in moderation.

Q. *When you specify "plenty of steak," can I eat over a pound of steak, if I want?*

A. Your guideline is this: *Never overload your stomach!* If you do, you won't lose weight as rapidly.

Q. *When you list salad in a daily menu, can I pile my plate to overflowing?*

A. You can eat lots of salad greens with a dressing of lemon and vinegar, but beware of the rich dressings, sauces, potato salad, croutons, and other additions that tempt diners at help-yourself restaurant salad bars. And, I repeat, never overload your stomach, no matter what—that involves a special health danger.

Q. *When I eat "assorted cheese slices," can I eat any kind of cheese, including Brie and other rich cheeses?*

A. If you are losing weight rapidly on the Diet, then such indulgence is permissible. Otherwise, select low-fat cheeses.

Q. *When I eat vegetables on the Diet, should I use "organically-grown" vegetables? Is it better to eat "health foods"?*

A. It definitely is not necessary, but I have no objections if that is your preference.

Q. *When I eat cold cuts, roast lamb, chicken, and turkey, as listed in the Diet menus, is there a specific limit to the size of the portions?*
A. No, but be sure to trim off all visible fat and skin before eating. And, I can't say it too often—use your good sense and *don't overload your stomach!*

Q. *Just what do you mean by "assorted cold cuts," as listed for the Monday lunch?*
A. Choose your own assortment of cold meats, chicken, turkey, even cold fish. Some possibilities are cold beef, lamb, veal, lean ham—but always with all visible fat removed. Avoid processed meats such as bologna and salami.

Q. *Can I scramble my eggs in butter, margarine, or bacon fat?*
A. No; coat the pan with non-stick vegetable spray, or with a little chicken broth—no need for any fats.

Q. *When you specify tuna fish on the Diet, does it have to be water-packed?*
A. No, but if the tuna fish is oil-packed, pour off all the oil you can. Do the same with canned salmon. Then rinse in a colander or strainer under cold water and shake dry.

Q. *When I have tuna fish or canned salmon, can I cut celery into it?*
A. Yes, if it makes it tastier for you, add celery and carrots, chopped parsley, squeeze in some lemon or lime juice—use your creativity.

Q. *When the menu specifies "vegetables," are there any that are not permitted?*
A. Yes—avoid corn, peas, potatoes, lentils, and any beans, except green or waxed.

Q. *Does it matter if the vegetables I eat on the Diet are always fresh, or can I also eat canned and frozen vegetables?*

A. You may eat fresh (usually tastiest) or canned or frozen vegetables, hot or cold, raw or cooked, but be sure that the canned and frozen vegetables are packed with no sugar or fats or rich sauces added; check the ingredients on the label before buying.

Q. *May I use herbs, seasonings, and spices on my food on the Diet, and a little grated onion or minced parsley or such?*

A. By all means.

Q. *Can I sprinkle a little grated cheese on my scrambled eggs, salads, and vegetables?*

A. Yes, but the key words in your question are "a little." If you load the servings with cheese, you won't lose as rapidly. Again, use good sense—check your progress on the scale each morning.

Q. *May I have some pickle slices, or pickle relish and olives with lunch and dinner?*

A. Yes, *in moderation.* Limit yourself to four small olives or three jumbo olives of any type.

Q. *May I use some ketchup, chili sauce, cocktail sauce, and mustard on meat and fish and other servings?*

A. Yes—once more, use the additives *moderately.* If you like mustard to enhance various servings, try a little of the tasty varieties available, such as tarragon mustard. (See the mustard dressing recipe.)

Q. *Can I have as much lemon in my tea as I want?*

A. Yes, to your taste. You may also add a few mint or peppermint leaves, or other herbs, if you like.

Q. *Is it permitted to use a little milk or cream, or non-dairy creamer in my coffee or tea?*

A. No, none of them; they are all high caloric. Most dieters come to enjoy the rich flavor of good coffee and tea "straight," hot or iced.

Q. *I know that I'm not allowed to use sugar in coffee or tea, or in any servings, but is it all right to sweeten with honey?*
A. No, neither sugar, honey, maple syrup, molasses, nor any such sweeteners—all are high in carbohydrates. You may use noncaloric sugar substitutes.

Q. *Can I make up servings of my own recipes as long as I use the ingredients and foods listed for the meal, and don't add any fats and foods not specified?*
A. Yes, but be careful to observe the basic SMD rules. For example, for Sunday lunch, you might combine the chicken or turkey with the listed vegetables and some instant chicken broth (or your own consommé with fat removed) in a delicious stew—remove all the skin and visible fat before cooking. Remove surface fat from the stew before serving.

As another example, for Wednesday dinner, in hot weather, if you're in a salad mood, you might cut up chunks of cold lamb with the salad fixings and create a deluxe salad.

By all means, use your culinary know-how and ingenuity. It will add to the joy of weight reduction.

Q. *When I'm on the Scarsdale Medical Diet, and can't have an alcoholic drink, is there a special non-alcoholic drink I can enjoy, particularly at a cocktail lounge or bar, or at a party?*
A. Yes, a number of dieters are enjoying what is becoming known all over as the "Scarsdale Special Highball." It's easy to mix—just plain soda (domestic or imported brands), ice, and a chunk of lemon or lime in a tall, frosted glass. It's very dry and refreshing, and looks as alcoholic as a gin-and-tonic or vodka-and-tonic. Actually, it's the famous Gin Rickey without the gin. Or you can enjoy any of the no-sugar diet

sodas on the rocks, in an old-fashioned glass, or in a highball glass—perhaps diet lemon soda or ginger ale with a chunk of lemon or lime. It does help to be drinking *something* while others around you are sipping from their glasses.

Q. *Am I permitted to spread low-calorie or no-sugar jelly or jam on my toasted protein bread at meals where listed on the diet?*
A. No, don't use any such spread at all. I suggest again that you eat the plain, crispy toast in small bites, savoring the crunchiness and nutty flavor.

Q. *In my salads, where specified on the Diet, can I use any of the "low-calorie mayonnaise" substitutes?*
A. No, not permitted—look at the listing again; they are not on the Diet, *so don't use them.*

Q. *I'm losing weight rapidly—11 pounds in my first week on the Scarsdale Medical Diet, but a friend warns me that when you lose the extra weight, you also lose some strength, energy, and endurance. I feel great, but can he be right?*
A. He is wrong if the weight you are losing is excess fat and flab. These are a burden, not a source of energy. If you are at all doubtful, tell your friend to notice how lean the top professional tennis players are. Because they are not carrying excess pounds, they are able to compete continuously, playing strenuous matches that often go on for hours.

Many players through the years, I think especially of Billie Jean King and Martina Navratilova, and a number of men as well, achieved their top form and ability only after they had taken off excess weight. The flab had been an extra load, cutting down their energy, speed, and endurance.

Q. *You don't list any soups on the Diet—are they forbidden?*
A. No. Low-calorie soups such as consommé, no-

fat vegetable soup, onion soup, borscht (see Gourmet Diet recipe) are excellent, and I would encourage you to add them. They have not all been placed on the menus because they are apt to complicate the simple meals.

Q. *With foods like "plenty of steak" on the Scarsdale Diet menus, isn't this an expensive way of eating?*

A. No, not when you add up the cost of cakes, cookies, ice cream, other sweets and desserts, butter or margarine, extra snacks and courses, and other items that you normally eat—*not on your Scarsdale Diet.* Compare the cost of your food shopping lists for "usual" high-fat, high-carbohydrate, therefore, high-calorie meals—versus your costs on the Diet.

To cut your costs even more, you can switch to the Money-Saver Diet, Chapter 9, during your second two weeks of Scarsdale dieting—and thereafter, if you prefer.

Q. *What do you consider to be the most common poor eating habit?*

A. Eating bread and butter while waiting for the meal to be served. Look around any restaurant and you will see what I mean. *Are you an offender?*

Q. *Is it necessary or required that I must "clean my plate" of everything listed at every meal on the Diet?*

A. No, not at all, not at any time. Eat as much as you want; don't substitute anything not listed on the Diet; don't ever overload; and *never hesitate to leave food on your plate.* You don't have to eat everything listed on the Diet—*don't substitute!*

Q. *I enjoy home-baked bread. Have you a recipe for a Scarsdale protein bread?*

A. Here it is.

SCARSDALE HOME-BAKED PROTEIN BREAD

      1 cup warm water
      1 teaspoon dry yeast (1 tablespoon = 1 cake
        yeast)
      ½ teaspoon salt
      1 teaspoon sugar
      ½ teaspoon cider vinegar
      ¾ cup soy flour
      ¼ cup gluten flour
      1¼ cups whole wheat flour
      Standard small bread pan (7⅜ x 3⅝ x 2¼
        inches)

Pour water into mixing bowl. Sprinkle dry yeast on water and let stand until it dissolves (about 5 minutes). Mix in salt, sugar, cider vinegar. Sift thoroughly, then gradually add soy and gluten flours, then whole wheat flour.

Mix slowly until dough stiffens and does not stick to sides of bowl (you may use a food processor, following machine directions, for this step). Lightly flour a board, then roll out the dough on it. Knead well (about 5 minutes) until dough feels smooth and elastic. Coat bread pan with no-stick vegetable spray. Shape the dough to fit, set it into the pan, cover with dish towel and set in a warm place to rise to about the top of the bread pan (2 to 3 hours). Preheat oven to 325°. Bake bread for about 1 hour or until well browned.

Home-baked bread is denser than commercial, so cut thin slices, then toast. Keep in refrigerator.

6
... "What Do I Do Now?" ...
Scarsdale Keep-Trim Diet
To Stabilize Weight Loss

"Everyone Eats But Few Know Flavor"
—CONFUCIUS
"Chew, Chew, Chew!"
—TARNOWER

Successful Scarsdale Medical Dieters obviously want to know what they have to do after the first fourteen days. For instance: "I am looking and feeling much better, but want to lose 15 more pounds. Can I continue on the Scarsdale Medical Diet for two weeks right now?"

No—you cannot extend the two weeks of the Scarsdale Medical Diet to four consecutive weeks, for the reasons previously given. Furthermore, it is very important to be developing *good lifetime eating habits*. Switch to the "holding pattern" for the next two weeks —the Keep-Trim Program.

This is spelled out in detail. The instructions are simple and easy. Follow them religiously, and you will in all likelihood lose additional weight. Certainly there should be no increase.

If you analyze the Keep-Trim Diet, you will immediately realize that it follows the same principles as the two-week Scarsdale Medical Diet. It is *low fat, low carbohydrate,* but not as specific or confining—for the simple reason that I am trying to help you develop good dietary habits unknowingly and painlessly.

There is no doubt of its efficacy. Literally hundreds of my patients have found it to be effective. No calorie counting, no weighing of food—don't overload your stomach. Chew, chew, chew—observe the simple "No! No! List."

It is wise to continue filling in a Weight Chart daily,

similar to the one used for the first two weeks. You are not likely to see the dramatic weight loss that you had on the two-week Scarsdale Medical Diet, but you should see something similar to the following chart. This is the case history of a typical dieter on Keep-Trim Eating.

Mrs. K.M.—age 44, 5'6"—she weighed 153 pounds at the start of her Scarsdale Medical Diet. Two weeks later, she had lost 15 pounds and was down to 138 pounds. Her desired weight goal was 125 pounds. Here is her chart on Keep-Trim Eating:

	DAY 1	DAY 2	DAY 3	DAY 4	DAY 5	DAY 6	DAY 7
FIRST WEEK	138	139	138	137	138	137	136
SECOND WEEK	137	136	135	135	136	135	134

TOOK OFF 4 POUNDS ON KEEP-TRIM EATING

Your Guidelines for Keep-Trim Eating

The two weeks on the Scarsdale Medical Diet will not only reduce weight, but will also develop a simple type of "behavior modification." The menus have been low in fats and carbohydrates, and consequently low in caloric content.

If you are like most of the people who used the Scarsdale Medical Diet successfully, you have developed a desire for cleaner, lower-calorie, low-fat, low-carbohydrate foods—and an aversion to rich, overly sweet, high-fat meals. This certainly makes it easier to be on Keep-Trim Eating.

Your guidelines are very simple—there is a much wider range of foods—observe the simple list of DON'TS. Do not be impatient on the routine I recommend here; you will certainly reach your goal easily, comfortably, and safely.

In brief, the Keep-Trim Diet is as follows:

No! No! List

- No more than two slices of protein bread a day.
- No sugar—sugar substitute may be used.
- No potatoes, spaghetti, or similar flour-based foods.
- No dairy fats.
- No candy or desserts, except fruit or no-sugar gelatin dessert.
- Restrict your alcohol intake to 1½ ounces a day of hard liquor, *or* 4½ ounces of dry wine, *or* 8 ounces low-calorie beer; no regular beer or ale.
- Carrots and celery may be eaten at any time.

All-Important DON'TS

The DONT'S listed in the following, in detail, should answer any questions you may have:

1. *DON'T* use sugar; you may use sugar substitutes.
2. *DON'T* use cream.
3. *DON'T* use whole milk; use skim or low-fat milk, if you wish, in moderation.
4. *DON'T* eat ice cream, ice milk, frozen custard, sherbet, or any frozen products that contain sugar or milk fats.
5. *DON'T* eat cakes, pies, cookies, sugar jellies, jams, preserves.
6. *DON'T* eat candy or chocolate.
7. *DON'T* eat potatoes, rice, sweet potatoes, yams, lima beans, baking beans, kidney beans, avocado.
8. *DON'T* eat spaghetti, macaroni products, noodles, other flour-based foods.
9. *DON'T* eat sausage, bologna, salami, etc., or fatty meats.
10. *DON'T* eat sweet desserts made with sugar; you may enjoy no-sugar gelatin desserts in all flavors.

11. *DON'T* add rich dressings, mayonnaise, or other similar salad dressings.
12. *DON'T* use butter, margarine, oils, bacon fat, shortening, or any kind of fat in cooking, or as spreads or dressings.
13. *DON'T* eat peanut butter.
14. *DON'T* eat more than two slices of bread per day, preferably protein bread toasted.

Great Variety of DO'S on Keep-Trim Eating

Focus on the extensive list of fine foods you may enjoy on Keep-Trim Eating. You'll find that there is an infinite variety of delicious, satisfying foods.

The following is a basic list of foods for your choice on Keep-Trim Eating:

• *An alcoholic drink daily,* dry (not sweet), if desired —1½ ounces of hard liquor, or 4½ ounces of dry wine. You may have Scotch, bourbon, rye, Canadian whiskey, vodka, gin, dry rum, cognac and other dry brandies. No sweet cordials or liqueurs. No sweetened mixed drinks. A dry martini or dry Manhattan are okay, but not sweet cocktails like old-fashioneds or whiskey sours. No mixtures with sugar sodas; use "no-sugar" diet sodas or club soda instead.

All *dry* red, white, rosé wines, dry champagne, and dry sherry are fine. No port, sweet sauterne, or other sweet wines. Only low-calorie beer is permitted.

• *All lean meats,* hot or cold—beef, lamb, veal, lean ham and pork; always trim off visible fat before eating.

• *Chicken and turkey,* hot or cold, cooked in a variety of styles and recipes—not fried; always trim off skin and any visible fat before eating.

• *All types of fresh and frozen fish;* avoid those canned in rich sauces. Cook to your taste, but butter, margarine, oils, shortenings, or other fats should not be used in preparation.

• *All types of shellfish*—shrimps, scallops, lobster, oysters, clams, crab, are fine.

• *Eggs any style* (but no more than three a week) prepared without butter, margarine, oils, other fats; enjoy scrambled eggs, omelets, boiled, hard-cooked, poached, fried (in a little instant chicken broth, or a skillet coated with non-stick vegetable spray).

• *Cheeses*—low-fat cottage cheese, low-fat pot cheese, American cheese, cheddar, Swiss, camembert—in fact, practically any cheese.

• *Soups, consommé, bouillon,* with vegetables, meats, chicken, fish—without cream, whole milk, or fat.

• *Vegetables*—generous servings of your selection (see Scarsdale Vegetarian Diet, Chapter 10).

• *Fruits*—apples, oranges, pears, cherries, plums, grapes, grapefruit, melons, watermelon—any fruit you desire.

• *Fruit and vegetable juices may be enjoyed,* but only natural juices with no sugar added—apple, orange, grapefruit, and so on. No-sugar tomato juices and mixed-vegetable juices are fine.

• *Nuts may be eaten sparingly*—walnuts, cashews, pecans, many of your favorites.

• *Bread* is permitted on Keep-Trim Eating, but limit yourself to two slices per day, preferably protein bread. You may have other breads and rolls for a change, as long as you don't exceed the limitation and don't select any breads, rolls, or muffins with sugar content or coatings.

• *No-sugar jellies,* jams, preserves may be used in moderation.

• *Green salads,* almost any and every combination of greens you can imagine and in whatever quantities you wish is allowable, laced with low-calorie dressings (not more than 15 calories per tablespoon), or with lemon, vinegar, and non-oily mixtures. A delicious choice, for instance, is the recipe for Vinaigrette Dressing, or Mustard Sauce Henri, on the Scarsdale Gourmet Diet, Chapter 8.

• *Beverages,* hot or cold, as much as desired—coffee,

tea, no-sugar diet sodas. No sugar; you may use sugar substitutes. Skim or low-fat milk may be added to coffee and tea, if desired.

• *Condiments*—ketchup, cocktail sauce, mustard, horseradish, pickle relish, pickles, olives of all types, in moderation.

• *Herbs, seasonings, spices,* to your taste.

Use Your Imagination and Enjoy Keep-Trim Eating

Concentrate on the overwhelming variety of DO's in the Keep-Trim listings, rather than bemoaning the DON'Ts. Your two weeks on Keep-Trim will help to rid you of bad eating habits, promote trimness and a longer, healthier, more vigorous lifetime.

Eating out in restaurants and at dinner parties is easy and not restrictive. It's just a matter of using good sense to keep on Keep-Trim Eating. If you want lobster, for example, order broiled lobster instead of creamy, high-fat Lobster Newburg with its high-caloric sauce.

Instead of drenching the broiled lobster with butter, squeeze on fresh lemon—it will enhance rather than hide the delicious natural flavor of good lobster meat.

Similarly, eat your chicken boiled, grilled, or barbecued—rather than as high calorie Chicken à la King, for example. You can go right down the menu and pick whatever you are permitted on Keep-Trim Eating.

Order fish broiled "dry," rather than cooked with oil, butter, or margarine.

There is no need to feel deprived at any time. For dessert, instead of custardy, sugary pastries, enjoy the crisp freshness of fruit compote in natural juices—no syrup that destroys the delightful true flavors.

On Keep-Trim Eating, you should leave the table feeling comfortable—never feel that you have overeaten.

You are limited only by your imagination. For example:

• Low-fat cottage cheese is a fine "creative" food. Make use of it on the Diet. Mix in a blender with a small amount of skim milk and lemon juice to make a "sour cream" base for many imaginative combinations.
• Spoon the "sour cream" over asparagus, broccoli or fruit.
• Mix your imitation sour cream with chili sauce or ketchup and grated onion or garlic powder.
• Chop some pimiento into it for an unusual salad dressing.
• Plain low-fat yogurt with a slightly tangier flavor may be used in similar combinations or blended with the cottage cheese.
• Try cooking with low-fat cottage cheese (see recipe for Spinach Cheese Pie Olga in the Money-Saver Diet, Chapter 9). Combine low-fat cottage cheese and eggs with crabmeat, bits of lean ham, chicken, shrimp, seasoned to taste and baked into a quiche. Sprinkle grated cheese or crumbled protein toast on top for added flavor.
• Mix low-fat cottage cheese into minced clams or de-hydrated onion soup mix as a dip for vegetables such as carrot, celery, squash or turnip sticks.
• For a dip, mince radishes, cucumbers, carrots, celery, and onion and stir into seasoned cheese. Sprinkle paprika on top or mix in for a pink dip.
• Instant beef or chicken broth add interest to many recipes. Sprinkle over mushrooms with a little lemon juice before broiling or sautéing. You won't miss the butter or margarine this mix replaces.
• Stir broth into hot vegetables for added flavor.
• Another super diet aid is gelatin. Molds prepared of gelatin can enhance many diet foods. A beautiful accompaniment to a chicken or turkey dinner is a mold made of gelatin into which grated carrots and orange or lemon rind are placed—or use sections of mandarin

orange, grapes, banana slices and other fruits in a similar way. The possibilities are endless!

• Use your leftover chicken, turkey or meats in a mold —just dice them and combine with permitted vegetables or use alone.

• Another delectable combination is seafood, chopped celery, carrots, radishes, and sliced pimiento-filled olives in a gelatin mold.

• Add piquance to your gelatin mold by using tomato, vegetable or fruit juices as your liquid, instead of water.

Use good sense in choosing lower-fat foods even within the "permitted" listings. In enjoying cheeses, try a selection of the part skim-milk cheeses instead of whole-milk cheeses. Some of the best-tasting cheeses available today, domestic as well as imported, are part skim-milk.

Take time now and then to check the charts in Chapter 14. They can help you to choose the proper low-fat, low-carbohydrate foods.

I Recommend This Eating Philosophy to You

Let's face it—most overweight people *love to eat.* The very obese are often gluttonous. Few people really know how to *enjoy* their food.

The true wine connoisseur can teach us a great deal. He examines, admires or criticizes the robe and clarity of the wine. He sniffs delicately to evaluate bouquet. He never gulps the wine but sips, rolling a little over his tongue and palate, to fully savor the aroma and taste.

As with the food epicure, the wine connoisseur *respects* what he is tasting. Even the clinking of glasses is done traditionally, it is said, to involve the sense of hearing. He rarely consumes more than a glass of fine wine. It is *vin ordinaire,* not the great wine, that is drunk by the pint or litre.

In a similar way, the simplest dish should be viewed and treated with admiration and respect. A scrambled egg or a hamburger can be beautiful, and prepared exotically. Smell and taste can be fully appreciated only by thoroughly chewing each bite of food before swallowing. The true enjoyment is gone once the food leaves the mouth. Chew, chew, chew.

It has been my observation that the vast majority of overweight people just don't take the time to carefully chew and enjoy their food. As you eat, try to analyze what ingredients were used in preparation. Don't hesitate to ask whoever prepared the dish for the details. Your interest will flatter and encourage the cook to do her or his best every time.

Allow enough time for your meal, so that you can chew very, very, very thoroughly, and savor completely.

One of the world's great gourmets, a recognized food writer and authority, was asked how he managed to keep trim year after year, even when reporting and rating restaurants where he dined as part of his work. He said, "I enjoy a taste, and don't often eat the whole serving. No matter how good a dish or a meal may be, I never never overeat—if I did, with all the restaurants I cover worldwide, I'd be long dead."

In the following chapters on the alternate Scarsdale Diets, you will find recipes for many delicious dishes. You can enjoy them during your weeks on Keep-Trim Eating, and after you are at your desired weight. They are low in fat and carbohydrates, therefore low in caloric content. Here are just a few that you can look forward to enjoying:

• *Chicken Hawaiian*—Money-Saver Diet, Chapter 9 —a delicious way of preparing chicken without added fat.
• *Lobster á la Nage*—Gourmet Diet, Chapter 8— adapted from a lobster dish I enjoyed in Brussels, which I think is the gourmet capital of the world.
• *Cold Poached Fish Natalia*—Gourmet Diet, Chapter

8—very low in fat, carbohydrates and calories, high in protein and subtle flavor.
• *Baked Apple Oscar*—Gourmet Diet, Chapter 8 —a very tasty dessert, with no sugar added.
• *Ratatouille*—Vegetarian Diet, Chapter 10—no fat added, delicious hot or cold, as a main dish or side dish.
• *Veal Napolitane*—International Diet, Italian Day, Chapter 11—a gourmet combination you'll serve proudly to anyone.
• *Don't miss the sauces, dressings, marinades*—all low fat, low carbohydrates, low calorie, and delicious.

After your two weeks of Keep-Trim Eating, if you still need to lose more weight, go back on the Scarsdale Medical Diet, or any of the other Scarsdale Diets.

7
Scarsdale
Two-On–Two-Off Program:
Keep Trim
for Your Lifetime

One of the principal keys to the success of the Scarsdale Medical Diet is the Two-On–Two-Off program. As explained previously, this is simplicity itself. Here's all you have to do in order to get down to your desired weight swiftly and surely:

1. Start with two weeks ON the Scarsdale Medical Diet . . .
2. Then switch to two weeks OFF the Diet and on Keep-Trim Eating . . .
3. If you need to lose more weight, go back ON the Scarsdale Medical Diet or ON your choice of the other four diets listed in detail for you . . .
4. After two weeks ON one of the five reducing diets, switch again to two weeks OFF dieting and on Keep-Trim Eating once more . . .
5. Continue on this Two-On–Two-Off program until you are at your desired weight.

That's the simple Scarsdale Medical Diet plan on which so many thousands of formerly overweight women and men have finally managed to reduce successfully to their desired weight. Many had been overweight for as much as ten, twenty, and more years— most had failed in many attempts to take off the excess weight and keep it off, up to the time that they went on the Scarsdale Medical Diet plan.

Most of the successful dieters have not gone back to their previous style of eating which had made them fat in the first place. Having learned new eating habits on the Scarsdale Medical Diets, and then through their two-week periods of Keep-Trim Eating, they continued for the most part on Keep-Trim Eating guidelines.

At the times when the newly slim person—as you will be—indulges and starts gaining excess pounds again, as people tend to do on vacations, heavy-eating weekends, and special occasions, you have an ever-handy tool:

The Four-Pound Stop Signal

Remember the Four-Pound STOP Signal. Step on the scale unclothed first thing each morning, to check your weight. Any time you see the scale register four or more pounds over your normal weight, *you go right back on the Scarsdale Medical Diet . . . starting with Day 1.*

You will be back to your desired weight within a few days. If for some reason, such as an extended vacation, you gained a great deal, your solution once again is the Two-On–Two-Off program.

TYPICAL CASE HISTORY

The following is a typical case history of how people slim down to desired weight on the Scarsdale Lifetime Keep-Trim plan:

"The Scarsdale Diet Two-On–Two-Off program helped me lose 35 pounds of overweight in a way that I could never manage before. Previously I couldn't stay on a diet that went on and on, seemingly forever.

"I found the two weeks on the Scarsdale Medical Diet easy because I could look forward to a change in fourteen days. I was thrilled that by the end of that time I had lost 20 pounds.

"When I finished the Scarsdale Medical Diet, the two weeks on Keep-Trim Eating felt like normal eating to me. I didn't feel at all deprived—and I was delighted to see that I had lost three more pounds. At the end of two weeks, I was not only ready but eager to go back on the Diet to take off the rest of my over-weight, only 12 pounds to my goal.

"Back on the Scarsdale Medical Diet for two weeks, I achieved 'the impossible dream'—I took off the 12 pounds, and after years and years of 'feeling fat,' hating the way I looked, I was down to the slim, trim 118-pound figure of my early twenties.

"Now that I know how to reduce on the Two-On–Two-Off program, and have the Diets that work, you can bet that *I'll never be heavy again!*"

It is not unusual for people to maintain a good weight for years. Remember to weigh yourself first thing each morning and fill in the Scarsdale Medical Weight Chart. In losing 35 pounds, for example, on the Two-On–Two-Off program, your weight charts could look like this; it can be fun, give you satisfaction, and improve your health and looks.

GOAL: 35-POUND WEIGHT LOSS

FIRST TWO WEEKS . . . ON THE SCARSDALE MEDICAL DIET:

	DAY 1	DAY 2	DAY 3	DAY 4	DAY 5	DAY 6	DAY 7
FIRST WEEK	153	151	150	149	148	147	145
SECOND WEEK	144	142	140	138	136	135	133

TOOK OFF 20 POUNDS

SECOND TWO WEEKS . . . ON KEEP-TRIM EAT-ING:

	DAY 1	DAY 2	DAY 3	DAY 4	DAY 5	DAY 6	DAY 7
FIRST WEEK	133	132	132	133	132	131	132
SECOND WEEK	133	132	132	131	132	131	130

TOOK OFF 3 POUNDS

THIRD TWO WEEKS . . . ON THE SCARSDALE MEDICAL DIET:

	DAY 1	DAY 2	DAY 3	DAY 4	DAY 5	DAY 6	DAY 7
FIRST WEEK	130	129	127	127	126	125	124
SECOND WEEK	124	123	122	121	120	119	118

TOOK OFF 12 POUNDS

FOURTH TWO WEEKS . . . ON KEEP-TRIM EATING:

	DAY 1	DAY 2	DAY 3	DAY 4	DAY 5	DAY 6	DAY 7
FIRST WEEK	118	119	118	117	118	118	119
SECOND WEEK	119	118	118	119	118	118	117

MAINTAINED DESIRED WEIGHT
(LOST 1 POUND)

The following chart illustrates the 35-pound weight loss in a continuing way over the eight-week Two-On–Two-Off program:

This woman could have shifted in her third two weeks to the Scarsdale Gourmet Diet, Money-Saver, Vegetarian, or International Diets; she elected to repeat the basic Scarsdale Medical Diet because she found it so simple, pleasant, and effective.

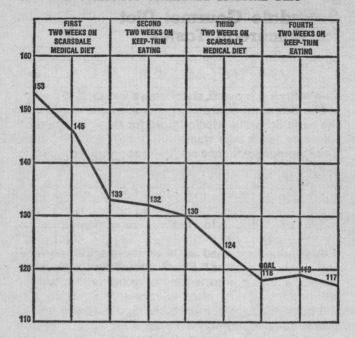

YOUR BASIC LIFETIME EATING PLAN

Keep-Trim Eating should become basic. As I mentioned, I personally follow it, and have for a great many years. Weighing myself every morning is a ritual I rarely miss. It indicates if and how much I can cheat.

For those who commit themselves to the Scarsdale Lifetime Keep-Trim plan, we have provided in Chapter 14 a calorie chart which lists a great many foods, with a breakdown of the percentage of protein, fat, and carbohydrate they contain. It can be interesting and helpful.

Basically, however, the simple Scarsdale Two-On–Two-Off program is the only guide you need. *The program works.* Follow it! You'll be able to say with confidence, like many other successful dieters: *"I'll never be heavy again!"*

8
Scarsdale Gourmet Diet for Epicurean Tastes

Stop being a gourmand, start being a gourmet!

The Scarsdale Gourmet Diet is a special version of the basic Scarsdale Medical Diet for those of you with epicurean tastes who want more menu variation, even if extra preparation time and effort are required.

This diet was carefully designed to trim down the overweight gourmet. It parallels the structure of the basic Scarsdale Medical Diet. By following directions precisely, even a gourmet will lose on average a pound or more per day, up to twenty or more pounds in the two weeks on the diet.

A gourmet is defined as "a connoisseur of fine food and drink; an epicure." Don't confuse that with *gourmand*, "a person who is fond of good eating, usually indiscriminately and often to excess; a glutton." The gourmand tends to be overweight, overstuffed, often afflicted with indigestion and other ills.

The gourmet is discriminating, selective and can be trim if she or he eats moderately and avoids very rich, high-fat, high-carbohydrate foods. Fortunately you don't need them to eat well. The menus and recipes for the Scarsdale Gourmet Diet can be served with pride to your most discriminating guests. I hope at the end of each day on the Diet you may feel as an earlier gourmet once did:

> *Serenely fed, the gourmet would say,*
> *Fate cannot harm me, I have dined today.*

You may, if you wish, switch back and forth from Gourmet to regular Scarsdale Medical Diet, but if you switch on Tuesday, use the Tuesday meals on *either* diet.

Remember that you follow the same time sequence

on the Gourmet Diet that you do on the regular Diet, two weeks on, then two weeks on the Keep-Trim Program. If you want to reduce further, return to the Gourmet or basic Scarsdale Medical Diet for another two weeks. Keep the same Weight-Loss Chart and recheck the rules if you aren't losing weight as quickly as you think you should.

As a special bonus, you may have three ounces of *dry* wine with dinner daily if desired, but only on the Gourmet Diet.

Scarsdale Diets Basic Rules
(Repeated here for your convenience.)

1. Eat exactly what is assigned. Don't substitute.
2. Don't drink any alcoholic beverages.
3. Between meals you eat only carrots and celery, but you may have as much as you wish.
4. The only beverages allowed are regular or de-caffeinated coffee, black; tea; club soda (with lemon, if desired); and diet sodas in all flavors. You may drink them as often as you wish.
5. Prepare all salads without oil, mayonnaise, or other rich dressings. Use only lemon and vinegar, or the vinaigrette or mustard dressing in Chapter 8, or dressings in Chapter 10.
6. Eat vegetables without butter, margarine, or other fat; lemon may be used.
7. All meat should be very lean; remove all visible fat before eating. Remove skin and fat from chicken and turkey before eating.
8. It is not necessary to eat everything listed, but don't substitute or add. Indicated combinations should be observed.
9. Never overload your stomach. When you feel full, *STOP!*
10. Don't stay on the Diet more than fourteen days.

KEEP THIS 14-DAY PROGRESS CHART OF YOUR WEIGHT LOSS:

	DAY 1	DAY 2	DAY 3	DAY 4	DAY 5	DAY 6	DAY 7
FIRST WEEK							
SECOND WEEK							

TOOK OFF ___ POUNDS

BREAKFAST EVERY DAY
    ½ grapefruit or other fruit listed**
    1 slice of protein bread, toasted
    Coffee/tea (no sugar or cream or milk added, sugar substitute may be used)

** *Choice of Fruit for Breakfast Every Day:* Grapefruit may be replaced any day by any of the following fruits in season:
    ½ cup diced fresh pineapple
    or ½ mango
    or ½ papaya
    or ½ cantaloupe
    or a generous slice of honeydew, casaba, or other available melon

YOUR CHOICE: In your daily Scarsdale Gourmet Diet menus, recipes for dishes marked with an asterisk* appear at the end of the entire week's menu listing.

If you prefer on any day not to use the listed recipes for lunch or dinner, simply substitute the lunch or dinner *from the same day of the basic* Scarsdale Medical Diet in Chapter 4. As an example, you may use the SMD Monday Lunch instead of the Gourmet Monday Lunch, and so on for every meal any day.

Scarsdale Diets: Substitute Lunch

If you wish, you may substitute the following lunch for any lunch, any day, on the Scarsdale Gourmet Diet:

> ½ cup low-fat pot cheese or cottage cheese, on lettuce
> Sliced fruit, all you want, as exotic as you desire
> 1 tablespoon low-fat sour cream topping the fruit
> 6 walnut or pecan halves, chopped and mixed with the fruit, or sprinkled over the fruit
> Coffee/tea—blends of your selection/diet soda

The clean, fresh, natural flavors of all the fine foods listed make this a true gourmet treat every time you decide to enjoy this substitute lunch. It is what I eat for lunch practically every day, and I savor it thoroughly.

After Your First Week

Repeat the daily menus here for your second week on the Scarsdale Gourmet Diet . . . or, if you like, you may substitute the week's menus of the basic Scarsdale Medical Diet, or one of the other Scarsdale Diets.

MONDAY

Lunch:
> *Borscht Suzanne
> *Chef's Spinach Salad Gourmet
> 1 slice of protein bread, toasted
> Coffee/tea/demitasse

Dinner:
  *Deviled Shrimp, served over
  ¼ cup plain boiled rice
  ½ head lettuce, with
  *Vinaigrette Dressing
  ½ cantaloupe (or choice of fruit from "Breakfast Every Day" listing)[1]
  Coffee/tea/demitasse

TUESDAY

Lunch:
  Fresh Fruit Salad, as much as you want. May use pineapple, melon, orange or grapefruit segments, pear, blueberries, strawberries, apple, etc.—your choice. Sprinkle with chopped mint leaves and lemon juice, if desired. Serve on lettuce leaves, and you may add watercress.
  1 slice of protein bread, toasted
  Coffee/tea/demitasse

Dinner:
  Plenty of broiled steak, lean, all visible fat removed—broiled to your personal preference of rare to well done.
  *Celery au gratin
  ½ head lettuce with lemon and capers
  Coffee/tea/demitasse

----

[1] In all Scarsdale Gourmet Diet daily menus, any of the fruits listed for breakfast may be substituted for the fruit dessert specified on any lunch or dinner if you prefer; however, if no fruit dessert is specified, no fruit should be eaten.

WEDNESDAY

Lunch:

> *Tuna (or salmon) Salad Gourmet
> 1 slice of protein bread, toasted
> Strawberries or raspberries or blueberries in
>   season, with grated lemon peel
> Coffee/tea/demitasse

Dinner:

> *Lamb à la Provençale
> *Broiled Tomato Supreme
> Green beans, cooked
> Cucumbers, radishes
> Coffee/tea/demitasse

THURSDAY

Lunch:

> *Eggs and Chicken Livers, farm style
> Tomatoes, lettuce, celery, olives, Brussels
>   sprouts or cucumbers
> 1 slice of protein bread, toasted
> Coffee/tea/demitasse

Dinner:

> Consommé Madrilène
> *Baked Chicken Breasts Herman
> *Spinach Delight à la Lynne
> *Peach with raspberries
> Coffee/tea/demitasse

FRIDAY

Lunch:

> Assorted cheese slices or wedges (your choice
>   of fine domestic or imported cheeses)
> *Eggplant Italiano

Sliced tomato with Belgian endive
Coffee/tea/demitasse

Dinner—Choice of:

*Cold Poached Fish Natalia (red snapper, striped bass, or other available fish) with
*Mustard Sauce Henri

Or

*Lobster à la Nage
Cold diced fresh vegetables (carrots, cauliflower, celery, mushrooms, scallions, etc.), all you want
*Baked Apple Oscar
Coffee/tea/demitasse

SATURDAY

Lunch:

*Fruit Suprême
1 slice of protein bread, toasted
Coffee/tea/demitasse

Dinner:

4 raw oysters or clams, with lemon wedge
*Chicken Bake Samm
Tomatoes, lettuce, cucumber
*Vinaigrette dressing (see Monday recipes)
½ grapefruit
Coffee/tea/demitasse

SUNDAY

Lunch:

Sliced cold white turkey with tarragon mustard
*Salad Chinese style
½ broiled grapefruit sprinkled with chopped mint
Coffee/tea/demitasse

Dinner:
> Broiled filet mignon
> *Turkish Zucchini
> Celery, cucumbers, radishes
> Coffee/tea/demitasse

Scarsdale Gourmet Diet Recipes

Here, and in the following pages, are the recipes for the dishes starred* in the daily menus for the Scarsdale Gourmet Diet.

For your convenience, recipes in most cases are listed to serve one—except in cases where the basic food, such as a can of tuna fish or a chicken, is too much for one person.

Since the recipes make delicious gourmet dishes, you may wish to increase the amounts of ingredients to serve a couple, family, and guests.

MONDAY LUNCH

BORSCHT SUZANNE
> ½ cup instant beef broth
> ¼ cup finely shredded white cabbage
> ¼ cup cooked or canned diced beets (no sugar)
> 1 teaspoon chopped onion
> Salt and pepper to taste
> Pinch of oregano
> 1 teaspoon low-fat sour cream

Bring broth to boil, add cabbage. Simmer 15 minutes. Add beets, onion, salt and pepper. Simmer 10 minutes longer. Remove from heat, and add oregano. Chill, and float sour cream on top when serving.

Serves 1.

SCARSDALE GOURMET DIET 69

CHEF'S SPINACH SALAD GOURMET

  2 cups or more of raw spinach
  ⅓ cup of diced assorted cheeses such as Swiss, Gouda, Blue (total about 1½ ounces)
  4 raw mushrooms, sliced
  2 thin slices boiled ham, diced
  1 scallion, sliced
  1 tomato, cut into eighths
  Garlic salt to taste
  Pepper to taste
  Vinegar or lemon dressing

Toss all ingredients except tomatoes together; add tomatoes and dressing just before serving.

Serves 1.

MONDAY DINNER

DEVILED SHRIMP

  5 jumbo (or 7 large) uncooked shrimp, peeled and deveined
  2 tablespoons dry white wine
  1 tablespoon Dijon mustard
  1 clove garlic, crushed
  ¼ cup diced onion
  Salt and pepper to taste
  1 small whole tomato (peeled)
  ¼ cup chopped parsley

Coat a skillet with non-stick vegetable spray. Heat and add shrimps, sautéing on each side 2 minutes. Add wine, mustard, garlic, onion, and seasonings. Cover and cook at medium heat 10 minutes. Add tomato, breaking it up with a fork. Mix all together, cover again, and cook 10 minutes longer. Add parsley and serve immediately.

VINAIGRETTE DRESSING

  ½ cup red wine vinegar
  2 teaspoons grated onion
  2 teaspoons chopped parsley

2 teaspoons chopped pimiento
1 tablespoon chopped pickle or capers
1 tablespoon water
¼ teaspoon freshly ground black pepper
Salt and paprika to taste
½ clove crushed garlic (optional)

Shake all ingredients together in a jar or bottle with a tight top. This dressing may be used on any mixed green salad, on artichokes, etc.

Keep chilled.

TUESDAY DINNER

CELERY AU GRATIN

1 cup celery cut into 1-inch slices
¼ cup lean beef broth
1 egg yolk
Salt and pepper to taste
1 tablespoon grated cheese, such as Romano or Parmesan

Boil celery in water until tender. Drain thoroughly. Place the slices in an ovenproof dish. Mix broth and egg yolk with a whisk. Add seasonings. Pour over celery and sprinkle with cheese. Place under broiler until nicely browned.

WEDNESDAY LUNCH

TUNA (OR SALMON) SALAD GOURMET

1 6½- or 7-ounce can solid-pack tuna fish (or salmon) oil drained off and fish rinsed in colander under cold water
2 stalks (or more) celery, diced
1 hard-cooked egg, chopped
2 teaspoons tiny capers
½-inch strip pimiento, diced
1 teaspoon grated onion (optional)
1 tablespoon lemon juice (or more, to taste)
1 shake Tabasco sauce (or more, to taste)
Watercress or Bibb lettuce (or other available)
Radish rosettes, sliced cucumber, lemon wedge

Place chilled drained tuna (or salmon) in a bowl and flake it with a fork. Add celery, hard-cooked egg, capers, pimiento (onion, if used), lemon juice, and Tabasco sauce, and mix without crushing. Serve on bed of watercress or Bibb lettuce or other lettuce, and garnish with radish rosettes, sliced cucumber, lemon wedge.

Serves 2.

WEDNESDAY DINNER

LAMB À LA PROVENÇALE

    5 ounces very lean leg of lamb
    ½ cup beef broth
    1 garlic clove, crushed (or less, if preferred)
    ½ cup parsley, chopped and mixed with 1 tablespoon dry rosemary
    Salt and pepper to taste
    1 small red pimiento (packed in water or vinegar)

Preheat oven to 350°

Be sure all fat is trimmed from lamb. Pour ¼ cup beef broth in an ovenproof dish. Rub meat with garlic and herbs. Sprinkle with salt and pepper. Bake 20 to 30 minutes to taste. Pour remaining broth over meat. Bake 5 to 10 minutes longer. Slice pimiento very fine, and sprinkle over lamb. Serve hot.

Serves 1.

BROILED TOMATO SUPREME

    1 tomato
    Salt and pepper to taste
    1 tablespoon chopped parsley
    ¼ teaspoon tarragon
    Garlic powder to taste
    Chives

Cut tomato in halves. Sprinkle each half with salt and pepper, and turn open sides down on paper towels; let drain one hour. Turn over and spread mixed herbs over open halves, adding garlic powder to taste. Broil for 7 minutes. Sprinkle with chopped chives before serving.

Serves 1 or 2.

THURSDAY LUNCH

EGGS AND CHICKEN LIVERS, FARM-STYLE

2 eggs, well beaten
2 tablespoons chicken bouillon
2 chicken livers, membrane and fat removed
Onion salt to taste
Cayenne (red pepper), a pinch

Coat a skillet with non-stick vegetable spray. Cook chicken livers in bouillon until light pink inside. Remove and chop fine. Add to eggs, with salt and cayenne. Respray pan if dried out, and cook mixture, stirring with wooden spatula, until set as you like it.

Serves 1.

THURSDAY DINNER

BAKED CHICKEN BREASTS HERMAN

2 boned chicken breasts (about 1½ pounds)
½ teaspoon celery salt
½ teaspoon mixed herbs
1 cup bouillon
3 tablespoons dry white wine
½ teaspoon minced onion
½ teaspoon minced parsley
Paprika

Preheat oven to 350°

Remove all skin and visible fat from chicken breasts; cut lengthwise into halves. Rub chicken all over with mixture of the celery salt and mixed herbs. Place in baking pan. Combine bouillon, wine, onion, parsley, and generous dash of paprika, stir well, and pour over chicken. Cover pan with foil and bake 25 minutes. Remove foil, brush chicken with liquid in pan, and bake uncovered 15 minutes longer or until chicken is tender to the fork. Serve with juice.

Serves 3 or 4.

SPINACH DELIGHT À LA LYNNE

    1 package frozen spinach
    Chicken broth
    1 tablespoon grated onion
    2 tablespoons low-fat yogurt
    Seasoned salt

Prepare frozen spinach, substituting chicken broth for water called for in package directions. Drain thoroughly, pressing out liquid. Stir grated onion, yogurt and seasoned salt to taste into spinach. Heat 3 minutes and serve. If you prefer "creamed-type" spinach, chop in processor before serving.

Serves 2.

PEACH WITH RASPBERRIES

    1 whole medium peach in season, or 2 halves
        packed in water and well drained
    ½ cup raspberries in season, or packed in water
        and well drained
    1 teaspoon vanilla extract
    ½ packet artificial sweetener

If peach is fresh, cover with boiling water for 10 minutes, then peel. Keep aside. Mix raspberries with ½ packet artificial sweetener and vanilla extract. Let stand for 30 minutes. Pour over peach. Chill before serving.

Serves 1.

FRIDAY LUNCH

EGGPLANT ITALIANO

    ¾ cup parboiled diced eggplant, well drained
    4 large mushrooms, sliced
    1 tablespoon onion, minced
    Salt and pepper to taste
    1 tablespoon parsley, chopped

Coat a skillet with non-stick vegetable spray. Add diced eggplant, turning with a spoon until lightly browned. Add mushrooms and onion, salt and pepper. Cover, simmer for 15 minutes. Add parsley, heat 5 minutes longer. Serve piping hot.

Serves 1.

FRIDAY DINNER

COLD POACHED FISH NATALIA

      1 pound center cut fresh red snapper, striped bass, or other available fish, with bone

COURT-BOUILLON:

      1 cup white wine vinegar
      1 cup dry white wine
      1 stalk celery, cut up
      1 carrot, cut up
      1 sprig dill
      2 cloves
      3 whole peppercorns
      1 tablespoon salt
      1 teaspoon dry mixed herbs

Use small fish poacher, or saucepan just about wide enough to hold fish. Place a rack on bottom. Put fish in poacher, just cover with water, then remove fish and put aside. The depth of the water will now indicate how far up to fill saucepan with the court-bouillon. Pour out water and put all ingredients for court-bouillon into poacher, adding water to reach previous depth. Cover and boil 20 minutes. Wrap fish in cheesecloth to hold it together, and lower to rack in poacher.

When court-bouillon boils again, reduce heat to very slow simmer. Allow to poach 10 minutes for each inch of fish measured at its thickest point (20 minutes if 2 inches thick, 25 minutes if 2½ inches thick, etc.). Fish should flake easily with a fork when done.

Carefully remove from poacher, drain on paper towels, wrap in clear wrap or foil and refrigerate until chilled through. Remove cheesecloth, peel skin off fish, and serve with *Mustard Sauce Henri.

Serves 2.

MUSTARD SAUCE HENRI

¼ cup Dijon mustard
⅓ packet artificial sweetener
⅛ cup white wine vinegar
Salt and pepper to taste
¼ cup plain low-fat yogurt
¼ cup chopped dill

Mix all ingredients together. Yield is about ⅔ cup. Keep in tightly closed jar. Refrigerated, will keep 2 to 3 weeks. Delicious on cold vegetables or seafood.

LOBSTER À LA NAGE

1 cup cooked lobster meat
½ cup chicken broth
¼ cup diced celery
¼ cup chopped parsley mixed with
1 tablespoon fresh or dry dill
Salt and pepper to taste
1 egg yolk
¼ cup dry white wine
Pinch of cayenne

Bring chicken broth to a boil, add celery, parsley-dill mixture, salt and pepper. Turn heat down and simmer 10 minutes. Add lobster pieces. Heat 5 minutes. Mix egg yolk with wine and cayenne, and stir into hot mixture. Serve immediately.

Serves 1.

BAKED APPLE OSCAR

1 medium baking apple
½ cup water mixed with 1 packet artificial sweetener
⅛ teaspoon ground cinnamon
Pinch of nutmeg

Preheat oven to 375°

Core and peel apple, leaving fruit whole. Place in a small baking dish. Pour flavored water around it. Bake for 20 minutes, then check to see if fruit is cooked through. It should be firm. Bake longer if necessary, then place under broiler for 2 minutes. Let cool to room temperature.

Serves 1.

SATURDAY LUNCH

FRUIT SUPRÊME

   ¼ fresh pineapple, cut lengthwise through leaf
      spikes (leave spikes on)
   ⅓ cup cubed or sliced mango (or papaya)
   1 plum, peeled and cut up
   ½ cup sliced strawberries
   ½ cup blueberries (in season) or ½ pear diced
   ⅛ cup pineapple juice
   1 tablespoon lemon juice
   Chopped mint leaves
   4 tablespoons cottage cheese

Remove meat from pineapple shell, reserving shell. Cut away core and put aside half the fruit for someone else. Cube the rest and mix with mango (or papaya), plum, strawberries, and blueberries (or pear). Spoon mixed fruit into pineapple shell, and pour pineapple and lemon juice over it. Top with cottage cheese and sprinkle with mint leaves. Serve chilled.

Serves 1.

SATURDAY DINNER

CHICKEN BAKE SAMM

   2½–3 pound chicken fryer, cut into eighths,
      all skin removed, fat scraped off
   4 tablespoons chicken bouillon
   ¼ teaspoon black pepper
   2 sprigs chopped parsley
   ¼ teaspoon oregano
   ¾ tablespoon garlic salt
   1 medium onion, sliced very thin
   1 pound fresh mushrooms, sliced
   3 tablespoons water
   2 tablespoons thinly slivered almonds

Place chicken pieces in shallow baking pan, brush with bouillon, and brown quickly on all sides 5 inches from broiler heat, turning often and keeping moist with bouillon. Remove from broiler, and sprinkle all over with pepper, parsley, oregano, and garlic salt. Heat oven to 350° (turn off broiler). Add onion, mushrooms, and water to chicken in pan, cover, and bake until chicken is tender and onions cooked through (about ¾ to 1 hour). Keep moist while baking, adding boiling water or bouillon if necessary. Sprinkle slivered almonds over top just before serving.

Serves 4.

SUNDAY LUNCH

SALAD CHINESE STYLE

    8–10 snow pea pods(fresh or frozen)
    6 asparagus tips (fresh, frozen or canned, drained)
    ¼ cup bamboo shoots (canned, drained)
    6 water chestnuts (canned) sliced
    ¾ cup Chinese cabbage, shredded
    4 mushrooms, sliced (or 2 ounces canned, drained)
    3 teaspoons lemon juice
    1 teaspoon soy sauce (no sugar added)
    ½ teaspoon dry mustard
    Minced parsley

In a saucepan with a little water, cook snow peas and asparagus tips (if fresh or frozen) in advance, until just heated through. Chill. Cut into bite-size pieces, and mix lightly with chilled bamboo shoots, water chestnuts, Chinese cabbage, and mushrooms. Combine lemon juice, soy sauce, dry mustard, and minced parsley, pour over salad and toss.

Serves 1.

SUNDAY DINNER

TURKISH ZUCCHINI
> 1 cup slightly undercooked diced zucchini
> ¼ cup minced onion
> ¼ cup diced tomato
> ¼ cup chopped parsley
> Salt and pepper
> ½ packet artificial sweetener
> 1 tablespoon shredded low-fat mozzarella
>   cheese

Lightly mix all ingredients except cheese. Pour into a small ovenproof dish. Sprinkle cheese over the top. Heat 10 minutes, 5 inches from broiler heat.
   Serves 1.

REPEAT THE DAILY MENUS for your second week on the Scarsdale Gourmet Diet.

After your two weeks on the Scarsdale Gourmet Diet, if you still want to lose more pounds to get down to your desired weight, go on to two weeks of Keep-Trim Eating. Following that, return to two more weeks on any of the Scarsdale Diets of your choice.

9
Scarsdale
Money-Saver Diet
To Save Pennies
and Lose Pounds

While lamb and steak conjure up visions of dollar signs, the Scarsdale Medical Diet is not "the rich man's diet." Many people find it costs substantially less to eat on the Scarsdale Medical Diet because the snacks, costly desserts, many other calorie-loaded "extras" that fill up the market bags and run up bills are missing.

Nothing is cheap in the market, but many of the staples in the Diet, like carrots, celery, zucchini, and so on, are among the most reasonably priced items to be found.

I have devised some Money-Saver recipes which illustrate how you can create imaginative, low-cost, low-fat, low-carbohydrate meals. They will help you to keep a very close eye on your budget. For example, you can economize on Saturday dinner by using the delicious recipe for Marinated Turkey Parts instead of roast turkey or chicken.

On this, as on the basic Diet, always follow the Scarsdale Medical Diet rules.

TIPS ON ECONOMY MEATS:

Check the best buys at markets, and be sure to select *lean cuts*.

One way to use less costly cuts of meat is to use a tenderizer, which contains enzymes from the papaya melon. Sprinkle tenderizer lightly and evenly on all surfaces, pierce meat all over with a fork, and allow to stand about a half-hour at room temperature before cooking. Salt is unnecessary when meat tenderizer is used.

If the tenderizer you choose is already seasoned, additional seasoning may not be needed. Follow instructions on package.

Meats may also be tenderized by *marinating*, which can add a variety of flavors, depending on which marinade mixture is used (see marinade recipes later in this chapter). The meat should be just covered with the marinade . . . placed in a covered container . . . kept in the refrigerator for at least an hour, or even overnight, turned occasionally.

Scarsdale Diets Basic Rules
(Repeated here for your convenience.)

1. Eat exactly what is assigned. Don't substitute.
2. Don't drink any alcoholic beverages.
3. Between meals you eat only carrots and celery, but you may have as much as you wish.
4. The only beverages allowed are regular or decaffeinated coffee, black; tea; club soda (with lemon, if desired); and diet sodas in all flavors. You may drink them as often as you wish.
5. Prepare all salads without oil, mayonnaise, or other rich dressings. Use only lemon and vinegar, or the vinaigrette or mustard dressing in Chapter 8, or dressings in Chapter 10.
6. Eat vegetables without butter, margarine, or other fat; lemon may be used.
7. All meat should be very lean; remove all visible fat before eating. Remove skin and fat from chicken and turkey before eating.
8. It is not necessary to eat everything listed, but don't substitute or add. Indicated combinations should be observed.
9. Never overload your stomach. When you feel full, *STOP!*
10. Don't stay on the Diet more than fourteen days.

KEEP THIS 14-DAY PROGRESS CHART OF YOUR WEIGHT LOSS:

	DAY 1	DAY 2	DAY 3	DAY 4	DAY 5	DAY 6	DAY 7
FIRST WEEK							
SECOND WEEK							

TOOK OFF ____ POUNDS

Scarsdale Diets Substitute Lunch

If you wish, you may substitute the following lunch for any lunch, any day, on the Scarsdale Money-Saver Diet:

> ½ cup low-fat pot cheese or cottage cheese, on lettuce
>
> Sliced fruit, all you want, best local market buys
>
> 1 tablespoon low-fat sour cream topping the fruit
>
> 6 walnut or pecan halves, chopped and mixed with the fruit, or sprinkled over the fruit
>
> Coffee/tea/diet soda

After Your First Week

Repeat the daily menus here for your second week on the Scarsdale Money-Saver Diet . . . or, if you like, you may substitute the week's menus of the basic Scarsdale Medical Diet, or one of the other Scarsdale Diets.

BREAKFAST EVERY DAY

> ½ grapefruit or cantaloupe or fruit in season (choose whatever costs least)

1 slice of protein bread, toasted; no spread added

Coffee/tea (no sugar, cream or milk added; sugar substitute may be used)

MONDAY

Lunch:

Chicken bouillon

*Chef's Salad

1 slice protein bread, toasted

Coffee/tea

Dinner:

Fish, fresh or frozen (depending on cost), broiled or baked

Combination salad (as many greens and vegetables as you wish)

½ grapefruit, or fruits in season

Coffee/tea

Recipes for starred* dishes are provided after the Sunday and substitute lunch menu listings.

TUESDAY

Lunch:

Fruit salad; any combination of fruits, as much as you want, on lettuce

Coffee/tea

Dinner:

Plenty of broiled lean hamburger (inexpensive cut; if possible, chopped at home after removal of all visible fat)

Brussels sprouts, in season, or cabbage or broccoli

Salad of lettuce, cucumbers, celery, radishes

Coffee/tea

WEDNESDAY

Lunch:

Tuna fish or salmon salad (oil drained off, as instructed earlier) with lemon and vinegar dressing, on lettuce
Grapefruit or melon
Coffee/tea

Dinner:

*Lamb Stew

Or

*Braised Lamb Shanks
Sauerkraut
Salad of lettuce, tomatoes, cucumbers, celery
Coffee/tea

THURSDAY

Lunch:

2 eggs, any style (no fat used in preparing)
Low-fat pot cheese or cottage cheese
Zucchini
1 slice protein bread, toasted
Coffee/tea

Dinner:

Boiled, broiled, roasted, or barbecued chicken, all you want; skin and all visible fat removed before eating

Or

*Broiled Chicken Hawaiian
Plenty of spinach
Coffee/tea

FRIDAY

Lunch:

>*Spinach Cheese Pie Olga
>No-sugar-added applesauce
>Coffee/tea

Dinner:

>Fish, any kind, fresh or frozen, broiled or baked, or sautéed or poached
>Combination salad, any fresh vegetables you want, including cold diced cooked vegetables if you prefer
>1 slice protein bread, toasted
>Coffee/tea

SATURDAY

Lunch:

>Fruit salad on lettuce, any kind of fruit you want, best market buys
>Coffee/tea

Dinner:

>Turkey or chicken, roasted, boiled, or broiled
>>Or
>*Marinated Turkey Parts
>Salad of tomatoes and lettuce
>Grapefruit or cantaloupe or watermelon
>Coffee/tea

SUNDAY

Lunch:

>Cold or hot turkey or chicken
>>Or
>*Broiled Chicken Hawaiian
>>Or

*Marinated Turkey Parts
Tomato, carrots, cooked cabbage (or broccoli
    or cauliflower, if preferred)
Coffee/tea

Dinner—Choice of:
*Broiled or Grilled Round Steak
Or
Cubed steak, pan-broiled in non-stick skillet
Or
*Boneless Ham
Or
*Liver and Onions
Or
*Lean Pot Roast (low-cost lean cut of meat,
    marinated and potted)
Or
*Tenderized Pimiento Steak
Salad of lettuce, cucumbers, celery
Cooked tomatoes (fresh or canned without
    sugar or oil) or Brussels sprouts
Coffee/tea

SUBSTITUTE LUNCH

Remember—because it is so delicious—that you may
substitute the following for lunch:

½ cup low-fat pot cheese or cottage cheese, on
    lettuce
Sliced fruit, all you want, best market buy
1 tablespoon low-fat sour cream, topping or
    mixed with the fruit
6 walnut or pecan halves, chopped and mixed
    with or sprinkled over the fruit
Coffee/tea/diet soda

After Your First Week

Repeat the daily menus here for your second week on
the Scarsdale Money-Saver Diet . . . or, if you like,

you may substitute the week's menus of the basic Scarsdale Medical Diet, or one of the other Scarsdale Diets.

Recipes

MONDAY LUNCH

CHEF'S SALAD

> Mixed greens of your choice (lettuce, escarole, Chinese cabbage, raw spinach, etc.)
>
> ½ cup strips of cold lean chicken or turkey or leftover lean meats, or a mixture of all three
>
> 1½-inch cube (or equivalent amount) of semi-hard cheese such as American, brick, cheddar, Jack, etc., or in combination
>
> ½ cucumber, sliced (optional)
>
> 3 radishes, sliced (optional)
>
> 1 slice green pepper, diced (optional)

Toss all ingredients together with choice of vinaigrette (see Gourmet Diet recipes, Chapter 8), vinegar, or lemon dressing.

> Serves 1.

WEDNESDAY DINNER

LAMB STEW

> 1½ pounds stewing lamb (be sure to look for leanest possible cut), all visible fat trimmed off, cut into 1½-inch pieces
>
> 2 carrots, cut in 1-inch slices
>
> 2 medium onions, sliced
>
> 2 green peppers, sliced
>
> 2 large tomatoes, chopped (or canned tomatoes drained, about 10 ounces)
>
> 1 teaspoon seasoned salt (or to taste)
>
> Black pepper to taste

Note: This recipe should be prepared in advance, cooled, and all fat that rises to top removed before reheating.

Quickly broil lamb pieces on all sides under broiler. Place in saucepan with vegetables and seasonings. Cook, covered, over slow heat one hour, or until lamb is tender. If stew becomes dry, add a little tomato juice or bouillon while cooking.

Serves 4.

BRAISED LAMB SHANKS

This cut of lamb is often fatty. Select shanks as lean as possible, and it is suggested that this recipe be prepared in advance so that it can cool and fat can be removed before reheating.

2 lamb shanks with all visible fat cut off

Use Scarsdale Diets Ketchup Marinade for Lamb and Poultry (see recipe, this chapter). Wipe lamb shanks with damp paper towel, place in marinade in heavy skillet. Refrigerate for 2 or 3 hours, turning lamb occasionally. Remove lamb from marinade and place under broiler, turning until all sides are browned. Return lamb to marinade in skillet, cover, and cook 1½ to 2 hours until lamb is very tender, basting with juices occasionally. Remove any visible fat. Uncover, and continue cooking 15 minutes. Let cool, and again remove fat. Reheat to serve.

Serves 2 to 3.

THURSDAY DINNER

HAWAIIAN MARINADE FOR CHICKEN

½ cup white wine or ½ cup white wine vinegar
1 cup prune juice
1 teaspoon grated orange rind
3 tablespoons lemon juice
1 teaspoon grated lemon rind
1 teaspoon salt
⅛ teaspoon pepper

Heat all ingredients to a boil. Remove from heat and let cool. Pour over chicken parts and refrigerate for an hour or two. Broil chicken at least 5 inches from heat, 15 or 20 minutes on each side, depending on size of chicken. Brush with marinade 3 or 4 times while broiling.

FRIDAY LUNCH

SPINACH CHEESE PIE OLGA

        2 10-ounce packages frozen chopped spinach
        3 eggs, beaten
        6 ounces low-fat pot cheese
        2 slices protein bread, dipped in water and then
            squeezed out
        ⅛ cup grated Parmesan cheese

Preheat oven to 375°. Thaw spinach and squeeze out water. Salt to taste. Add other ingredients, breaking up wet bread with a fork, and mix all together evenly. Press lightly into bottom of 9-inch pie pan (use a non-stick pan or coat well with no-stick vegetable spray). Bake approximately 40 to 45 minutes. Center should be slightly firm and edges a little brown. (Freezes well —wrap carefully. Thaw before reheating and serving.)
    Serves 3 or 4.

SATURDAY DINNER
(Or Sunday Lunch, or both)

MARINATED TURKEY PARTS

        2 turkey drumsticks, if frozen, thaw, or
        2 turkey wings or 2 turkey thighs

Use Lemon Marinade for Lamb or Poultry (recipe, this chapter). Wipe turkey parts with damp paper towel, trim off fat and superfluous skin, and place in baking pan just large enough to hold turkey in one layer. Pour marinade over turkey parts, refrigerate about 2 hours or overnight. Turn parts occasionally and brush with marinade to keep moist and flavored (we often wonder whether cooks get up during the night to turn marinating foods!). About 2 hours before dinner, heat oven to 350°, remove turkey from pan, pour off marinade into a bowl, and place rack in pan. Lay turkey on rack and roast for 2 hours, turning every ½ hour and brushing with marinade. More, or less, roasting time may be needed, depending on size of parts. Wings will take less time than drumsticks or thighs.

Serves 2.

SUNDAY DINNER

BROILED OR GRILLED ROUND STEAK

    2 pounds top round steak, all visible fat removed

MARINADE:

    2 small onions, chopped

    ¼ cup lemon juice

    ½ cup wine vinegar

    ¼ cup unsweetened soy sauce

    1 tablespoon Worcestershire sauce

    1 garlic clove, minced, or ½ teaspoon garlic powder (or more, if you like garlic)

    1 teaspoon salt

Shake together in covered jar all ingredients for marinade. Allow to stand 2 or 3 hours to combine flavors. Place meat in shallow dish and pour marinade over it to tenderize it. Refrigerate for 2 or 3 hours, turning meat occasionally. Broil or grill meat to desired doneness 5 inches from heat, turning 3 or 4 times and brushing each time with marinade. Serve cut into thin, diagonal slices.

Serves 4.

BONELESS HAM

    1 3-pound tin fully cooked boneless ham

    2 ounces orange juice

    2 tablespoons dry mustard

Trim all possible fat from ham. Place in small baking pan coated with no-stick vegetable spray. Combine orange juice with dry mustard and spread over exposed surfaces of ham. Bake in 350° oven until heated through (about ½ to ¾ hour, depending on thickness). Serve thinly sliced. Put aside any fat exposed while eating.

Serves 8.

LIVER AND ONIONS

  1 pound calves or beef liver, ¼ inch thick, cut
    into thin strips
  2 medium onions, sliced
  3 tablespoons beef bouillon
  Seasoned salt
  Pepper
  Grated Parmesan or Romano cheese

Remove veins and outer skin of liver and wipe with
damp paper towels before cutting into strips. Coat a
skillet with no-stick vegetable spray. Sauté onions in
bouillon until transparent. Add liver strips, salt and
pepper, and cook, stirring, until liver is browned
(about 3 minutes). Sprinkle with grated cheese before
serving.
  Serves 2 to 3.

PIMIENTO STEAK (Tenderized)

  2½ pounds blade chuck steak (look for lean
    cut, then remove all visible fat)
  Meat tenderizer (not over 1 year old)
  1 large onion, sliced
  2 green peppers cut into thin circles
  1 small can pimientos, chopped
  1 clove garlic, crushed
  Juice of 1 lemon
  Salt
  Pepper

Sprinkle steak with tenderizer and pierce all over with
fork. Allow to stand about ½ hour (or follow instructions on tenderizer package). Cut meat into ½-inch
strips, removing any more fat as you do so. Sprinkle a
little salt over onion and peppers and cook together
in a skillet coated with no-stick vegetable spray, until
tender and brown. Add steak slices and pimiento, turning as mixture cooks 3 minutes. Add garlic and lemon
juice, continue cooking and stirring for about 3 minutes
longer.
  (When using tenderizer on meats, be certain it has

not been on the shelf too long, since the enzymes it contains lose their potency in a year or two.)

Serves 6.

OVEN-BRAISED BEEF (Pot Roast)

    3 pounds boneless beef chuck top roast, all visi-
      ble fat removed
    1 medium onion, sliced thin
    2 carrots, sliced thin
    1 rib celery, sliced thin
    1 cup dry red wine (or tomato juice)
    1 tablespoon tomato paste
    1 clove garlic, crushed
    1 teaspoon thyme
    3 sprigs parsley
    1 bay leaf
    2 whole cloves
    1 tablespoon cornstarch

Marinate meat in your choice of Money-Saver Diet marinades for several hours, turning occasionally. Place marinated beef in center of large piece of heavy duty foil lining a roasting pan. Place under broiler, turning till all sides of meat are browned. Turn off broiler heat. Place sliced onion, carrots, and celery around meat. Mix together wine (or tomato juice), tomato paste, parsley, garlic, thyme, bay leaf, and cloves, and pour over the meat. Roast in 325° oven 2½ to 3 hours, until fork pierces meat easily. Remove meat and vegetables from foil, discard bay leaf and cloves; strain liquid into a saucepan and skim off fat. Mix cornstarch with 1 tablespoon water and stir into strained juice. Cook gently, stirring, until slightly thickened. Allow to cool completely, and again skim off fat. To serve, slice meat thin and surround with vegetables, pour thickened juices over and reheat.

Serves 7 to 8.

MARINADES FOR BEEF

BEEF TARRAGON MARINADE
¾ cup tarragon vinegar
1 medium onion, chopped
1 carrot, chopped
4 sprigs parsley
1 bay leaf
1½ teaspoon garlic salt
½ teaspoon black pepper
3 drops Tabasco sauce

BEEF WINE MARINADE
¾ cup dry red (or white) wine
1 onion, minced
½ cup chopped parsley
½ teaspoon tarragon
½ teaspoon thyme
1½ teaspoons garlic salt (or plain salt, if garlic
    not desired)
1 bay leaf
Dash red pepper

MARINADES FOR LAMB OR POULTRY

LEMON MARINADE
¾ cup wine vinegar
3 tablespoons lemon juice
1 medium onion, minced
1 clove garlic, crushed
¼ cup chopped parsley
1 bay leaf
⅛ teaspoon thyme
⅛ teaspoon tarragon
2 teaspoons salt
½ teaspoon pepper

KETCHUP MARINADE
> ½ cup vinegar
> 2 onions, sliced
> 1 cup water
> 2 tablespoons Worcestershire sauce
> 1 cup ketchup
> 1 packet sugar substitute
> 1 teaspoon dry mustard
> 1½ teaspoons salt
> ½ teaspoon pepper

MINT MARINADE
> 1 cup wine vinegar
> 1 onion cut in eighths
> 8 whole cloves
> 2 cloves garlic, crushed
> 2 teaspoons salt
> ¼ teaspoon black pepper
> 4 sprigs parsley
> 2 sprigs mint (or 1 teaspoon chopped dried mint)
> ⅛ teaspoon thyme
> 1 teaspoon lemon rind (optional)

(Can be strained and used for sauce for lamb after cooking.)

MISCELLANEOUS MARINADES

RED *MEAT* MARINADE (for single serving)
> ½ cup instant beef broth
> 1 tablespoon cider vinegar
> 1 garlic clove, or 1 tablespoon cider vinegar
> Salt and pepper to taste
> 1 tablespoon chopped parsley
> (If desired, you may add 1 tablespoon soy sauce.)

WHITE WINE *POULTRY* MARINADE

        ½ cup instant chicken broth (fat drained off)
        1 tablespoon dry white wine
        ⅛ teaspoon celery seeds
        1 teaspoon herbs such as oregano, tarragon,
            parsley
    Salt and pepper to taste

FENNEL *FISH* MARINADE

        ¼ cup instant chicken broth (fat drained off)
        2 tablespoons lemon juice
        1 teaspoon fennel seeds
        ⅛ teaspoon ground coriander
    Salt and pepper to taste

Marinade Directions: Mix all ingredients. Pour over meat, poultry, or fish. Let meat or poultry stand 2 to 3 hours, turning occasionally. Let fish stand 1 to 2 hours, turning occasionally.

REPEAT THE DAILY MENUS for your second week on the Scarsdale Money-Saver Diet.

After your two weeks on the Scarsdale Money-Saver Diet, if you still want to lose more pounds to get down to your desired weight, go on to two weeks of Keep-Trim Eating. Following that, return to two more weeks on any of the Scarsdale Diets of your choice.

10
Scarsdale Vegetarian Diet

The Scarsdale Vegetarian Diet is based on vegetables, fruits, some dairy products, nuts, and limited amounts of grains. I know that there are many types of "vegetarians." Some eat only "nonflesh" items. Others will also eat eggs and dairy products . . . or eggs or dairy products, but not both . . . there are dozens of variations.

I suggest that you adapt this basic Vegetarian Diet to your personal choice. Observe the basic Scarsdale Diet rules as they apply to you. *Never overload your stomach.* Keep a daily weight chart.

You should lose about a pound a day on average, up to 20 or more pounds in the fourteen days on the Scarsdale Vegetarian Diet.

Follow the Diet for two weeks, then use and vary Keep-Trim Eating according to your vegetarian regulations.

Many vegetarians use cookies, cake, chocolate, and other sweets—*avoid them like Satan!*

Scarsdale Diets Basic Rules Adapted for the Vegetarian Diet

1. Eat exactly what is assigned. Don't substitute.
2. Don't drink any alcoholic beverages.
3. Between meals you eat only carrots and celery, but you may have as much as you wish.
4. The only beverages allowed are regular or decaffeinated coffee, black; tea; club soda (with lemon, if desired); and diet sodas in all flavors. You may drink them as often as you wish.
5. Prepare all salads without oil, mayonnaise, or other rich dressings. Use only lemon and vinegar, or the

95

vinaigrette or mustard dressing in Chapter 8, or dressings in Chapter 10.
6. Eat vegetables without butter, margarine, or other fat; lemon may be used.
7. It is not necessary to eat everything listed, but don't substitute or add. Indicated combinations should be observed.
8. Never overload your stomach. When you feel full, *STOP!*
9. Don't stay on the Diet more than fourteen days.

KEEP THIS 14-DAY PROGRESS CHART OF YOUR WEIGHT LOSS:

	DAY 1	DAY 2	DAY 3	DAY 4	DAY 5	DAY 6	DAY 7
FIRST WEEK							
SECOND WEEK							

TOOK OFF ___ *POUNDS*

Vegetables Not Permitted on Scarsdale Vegetarian Diet

• Avocados
• Dry beans (baked beans, lentils, dry white beans, red kidney beans, lima beans, chick peas, black-eyed peas, etc.; except soybeans, which are permitted in the Vegetarian Diet)
• Sweet potatoes
• Yams

• Where protein bread is unavailable, gluten bread or whole wheat bread may be substituted.
• Neither cream cheese nor farmer cheese is permitted. Use no milk, no cream, no nondairy creamer (skim and low-fat milk permitted in moderation). No butter,

no margarine, no yogurt or sour cream except *low-fat* where indicated on the Vegetarian Diet.
• No noodles, spaghetti, or similar starchy foods. No cereals, no bread products except as stated above.
• No cakes, cookies, candies, ice milk, sherbet, ice cream; no sweets of any kind.
• No meats, fowl, fish, shellfish, or eggs on this Vegetarian Diet.
• No oils or other fats or mayonnaise except no-stick vegetable spray for cooking.

Substitute Meals Permitted

Any day, for lunch or dinner, you may substitute for menus in this chapter a hot or cold vegetable plate, any vegetables you like and as many as you like—except for those not permitted, mentioned in the opening of this chapter.

Accompany vegetables with one baked potato sprinkled with salt and chives, if desired. Or, ½ cup boiled rice may be substituted for potato. Or 1 slice protein bread, toasted, with no-sugar jam or jelly, if desired. Or, you may have 4 ounces cooked soybeans instead (weighed after cooking; 1 ounce uncooked).

On salads, you may use lemon or vinegar or any of the Scarsdale Diet Dressings (see recipes that follow the Vegetarian menus).

Scarsdale Diets: Substitute Lunch

If you wish, you may substitute the following lunch for any lunch, any day, on the Scarsdale Vegetarian Diet:

     ½ cup low-fat pot cheese or cottage cheese
     Sliced fruit, all you want
     1 tablespoon low-fat sour cream topping or mixed with the fruit

6 walnut or pecan halves, chopped and mixed with the fruit or sprinkled over the fruit
Coffee/tea/herb tea/diet soda

BREAKFAST EVERY DAY

½ grapefruit or other fruit in season
1 slice protein bread, toasted, spread with no-sugar jam or jelly, if desired
Tea/coffee/herb tea (no sugar, cream or milk)

MONDAY

Lunch:

*Watercress (or broccoli) soup
Baked potato with low-fat cottage cheese and chives

Or

1 ounce uncooked or 4 ounces cooked soy-beans (weighed after cooking)
6 halves of walnuts or pecans
*Baked Apple Oscar (see recipe, Gourmet Diet, Chapter VIII)
Tea/coffee/herb tea

Dinner:

2 slices cheese of your choice on lettuce
*Ratatouille
Artichoke hearts (no oil!), cucumbers, radishes
1 slice protein bread, toasted
Cantaloupe or watermelon or sliced orange
Tea/coffee/herb tea

TUESDAY

Lunch:

Fruit salad, as much as you want, any kind of fruit with lettuce, celery
1 slice protein bread, toasted, spread with no-sugar jam or jelly, if desired
Tea/coffee/herb tea

Dinner:
>   *Apple-Nut Acorn Squash
>   Hot or cold vegetables, cauliflower, carrots, to-
>   matoes, all you want
>   4 olives
>   Tea/coffee/herb tea

WEDNESDAY

Lunch:
>   *Stuffed Tomato
>   Broiled mushrooms, zucchini, and carrots
>   1 slice protein bread, toasted
>   Tea/coffee/herb tea

Dinner:
>   *Asparagus (or cauliflower or broccoli) Au Gra-
>   tin
>   *Hawaiian Fruit-Nut Squash
>   Green salad and tomatoes
>   1 slice protein bread, toasted
>   Tea/coffee/herb tea

THURSDAY

Lunch:
>   Low-fat cottage cheese with sliced scallions,
>   radishes, cucumbers
>   Olives
>   1 slice protein bread, toasted
>   Or
>   1 ounce uncooked or 4 ounces cooked soy-
>   beans
>   Apple
>   Tea/coffee/herb tea

Dinner:

>*Scarsdale Eggplant Parmesan
>Green salad with choice of *Scarsdale Diet low-
>   calorie dressings
>Fresh fruit cup with squeeze of lemon or lime,
>   minced mint leaves
>Tea/coffee/herb tea

FRIDAY

Lunch:

>Assorted cheese slices
>Spinach
>1 slice protein bread, toasted
>Peach or pear
>Tea/coffee/herb tea

Dinner:

>Onion bouillon, with *Protein Croutons
>*Stewed vegetables
>No-sugar applesauce with 6 walnuts or pecans
>Tea/coffee/herb tea

SATURDAY

Lunch:

>Fruit salad, any kind, as much as you want, with
>   low-fat pot cheese or cottage cheese, on let-
>   tuce or other greens
>1 slice protein bread, toasted
>Tea/coffee/herb tea

Dinner:

>*Vegetable Cheese Casserole served with
>   ½ cup no-sugar applesauce sprinkled with 1
>   tablespoon raisins
>Sliced tomato and lettuce with vinegar and
>   lemon dressing or *Scarsdale Diet Dressing
>Tea/coffee/herb tea

SUNDAY

Lunch:
> *Stuffed Tomato (see recipe for Wednesday lunch; using stuffing 3,); (no rice, no potato)
> Boiled or mashed potato (no butter) with 1 tablespoon low-fat sour cream and chives
> > Or
> 4 ounces soybeans, weighed after cooking
> Stewed fruit; use sugar substitute if wanted
> Tea/coffee/herb tea

Dinner:
> *Chow Mein on Rice
> Salad of lettuce, sliced tomatoes
> Sliced pineapple or pineapple chunks (if canned, packed in its own juice or in water, *not* sugar-sweetened syrup)
> Tea/coffee/herb tea

SCARSDALE DIET LOW-CALORIE DRESSINGS
(for use on any salads or cold vegetables)

MUSTARD SAUCE HENRI
(See Gourmet Diet Recipes, Chapter 8.)

WINE VINEGAR SALAD DRESSING
> 1 teaspoon dry mustard
> ½ cup wine vinegar
> 3 tablespoons water
> 1 teaspoon chopped capers
> 1 teaspoon minced parsley
> 1 teaspoon chopped pimiento
> 1 teaspoon seasoned salt
> Dash of pepper

Dissolve mustard in a little wine vinegar by rubbing with the back of a spoon. Put all ingredients in small covered jar and shake. Refrigerated, will keep for a long time.

LEMON-PAPRIKA SALAD DRESSING

        1 teaspoon dry mustard
        The juice of 4 lemons
        1 teaspoon paprika
        2 teaspoons minced parsley
        1 teaspoon chopped chives
        ½ teaspoon oregano
        1 teaspoon salt
        Shake of Tabasco sauce

Dissolve mustard in a little lemon juice by rubbing with the back of a spoon. Shake all ingredients together in a small covered jar. Refrigerate, and use as needed.

ONION SALAD DRESSING

        ½ cup wine vinegar
        2 teaspoons grated onion
        1 teaspoon salt
        ⅛ teaspoon lemon-pepper marinade seasoning
        ½ teaspoon dill
        ½ teaspoon minced parsley
        1 teaspoon water

Shake all ingredients together in a small covered jar. Refrigerate, and use as needed.

YOGURT SALAD DRESSING

        ½ small container yogurt
        2 shakes of ketchup

Stir together and use sparingly on salads or vegetables.

Recipes

MONDAY LUNCH

WATERCRESS SOUP

        1 bunch watercress, washed and trimmed
        1 cup plain low-fat yogurt
        1 envelope instant onion broth or bouillon mix
        Salt and pepper to taste

        1 cup water
        2 thin slices lemon
Purée all ingredients except water and lemon in a food
processor or blender. Pour into saucepan, add water
and seasonings (to taste), and bring just to boiling
point, stirring. Spoon into two soup bowls and float
a slice of lemon on each serving. Eat while piping hot!
    Serves 2.
    (This recipe may be prepared with broccoli, cabbage,
escarole, spinach, Swiss chard, etc., instead of watercress.)

MONDAY DINNER

RATATOUILLE
        2 medium onions, sliced thin
        2 medium green peppers, sliced thin
        1 large clove garlic, crushed
        1 medium eggplant, peeled and cut into ¾-inch
          cubes
        2 medium zucchini, cut crosswise into ¼-inch
          slices
        5 medium tomatoes, peeled and chopped
        ¼ cup parsley, chopped
        2 teaspoons salt
        Pepper to taste
        ½ cup sliced pimiento-stuffed olives
Coat heavy saucepan with no-stick vegetable spray.
Sauté onions, green peppers, and garlic until onions are
slightly cooked. Add all other ingredients except parsley, cover and simmer 25 to 30 minutes until vegetables
are crisp but tender. Stir in parsley and cook 5 to 10
minutes longer, until mixture reaches thickness you
like, stirring occasionally. Add olives. Serve hot or
chilled.
    Serves 4 to 6.

TUESDAY DINNER

APPLE-NUT ACORN SQUASH

1 acorn squash
½ teaspoon salt
1 medium apple, chopped
½ teaspoon lemon juice
5 whole pecans or walnuts, chopped
1 pecan or walnut, halved
1 teaspoon artificial brown sugar sweetener

Preheat oven to 400°. Cut acorn squash into halves lengthwise and scrape out seeds and fiber. Place halves in baking pan with cut sides down and pour ½-inch of water into pan around them. Bake 20 minutes, or until just tender. Pour off water. Sprinkle salt into squash halves, and fill them with a mixture of the chopped apple, chopped nuts, and lemon juice. Sprinkle sweetener over tops of filled halves. Return to oven and bake 10 minutes, or until filling is piping hot. Serve with ½ nut centered on each half.

Serves 1 or 2.

WEDNESDAY LUNCH
(and Sunday Lunch)

STUFFED TOMATO

2 large tomatoes
½ cup cooked rice
½ cup shredded American cheese
Salt and pepper to taste

Cut ½-inch off the tops of each tomato. Scoop out some of the tomato pulp, leaving about a ¾-inch thick shell. Mix other ingredients together and pack lightly into tomato shells, saving a little cheese to sprinkle on top of each stuffed tomato. Place in small baking dish and bake for 15 or 20 minutes in preheated 350° oven, or until piping hot. Do not overcook.

Serves 2.

Other stuffings may be used, as follows:

NO. 1

¼ cup cooked rice; ½ medium pepper, chopped; 4 large mushrooms, sliced and sautéed; ¼ cup shredded cheddar cheese (or other cheese).

NO. 2

½ cup cooked (or canned) corn; chopped tomato pulp; ½ medium pepper, chopped; ½ chopped pimiento

NO. 3

Cottage cheese and chopped nuts, topped with minced parsley

NO. 4

You may create your own from allowed foods.

WEDNESDAY DINNER

ASPARAGUS AU GRATIN (OR CAULIFLOWER OR BROCCOLI)

    6 to 8 spears of asparagus (or 1 to 2 cups cauliflower or broccoli pieces)
    ¼ cup shredded cheese (any kind that melts, preferably made of part skim milk)
    Protein croutons (see recipe in this chapter)

Prepare vegetable as usual (may be fresh, frozen, or canned). Melt cheese and pour over vegetables. Sprinkle croutons over cheese.

Serves 1.

HAWAIIAN FRUIT-NUT SQUASH

    1 package mashed squash, frozen (without butter), thawed
    ½ teaspoon salt, or more, if needed
    2 tablespoons low-fat sour cream
    ½ cup pineapple chunks, packed in water or own juice, drained

½ cup orange segments or Mandarin oranges, canned without sugar, drained

6 walnut or pecan halves, either chopped or whole

Chopped mint

Preheat oven to 350°. Beat together mashed squash, sour cream, and salt. Add pineapple chunks and orange segments. Put mixture into a small casserole and heat in oven for 15 minutes, or longer, until very hot. Place chopped nuts or nut halves on top of casserole. Sprinkle a little chopped mint on top, also.

Serves 2.

THURSDAY DINNER

SCARSDALE EGGPLANT PARMESAN

1 medium eggplant, cut in ¼-inch slices

10 to 12 ounces tomato sauce

2 teaspoons chopped parsley

2 teaspoons chopped chives (or 1 teaspoon grated onion)

4 tablespoons grated Parmesan cheese

1 teaspoon garlic salt

Shake of pepper

1 teaspoon crushed oregano

3 ounces part skim mozzarella cheese, cut into 8 to 10 thin slices

Place slices of eggplant into boiling, slightly salted water in large saucepan; turn down heat and simmer for 3 minutes. Drain off water and pat slices with paper towels to dry. Brown on both sides in large skillet coated liberally with no-stick vegetable spray (if you use two skillets at a time, process may not have to be repeated to brown all eggplant). Mix together tomato sauce, parsley, chopped chives (or onion), Parmesan cheese, garlic salt, pepper, and oregano. Cover the bottom of a shallow, medium-size (about 4 x 8 or 5 x 9) baking pan with a little sauce, cover with slices of eggplant, add ⅓ of mozzarella cheese, cover with sauce, then eggplant, then mozzarella cheese, etc., alternating layers. Top with remaining sauce and a sprinkle of Parmesan cheese. Bake in preheated oven (375°) 35 minutes, until very hot.

Serves 2 to 4.

FRIDAY DINNER

STEWED VEGETABLES

    1 cup chopped onions
    1 pound tomatoes
    1 teaspoon seasoned salt
    Dash of sugar substitute
    Pinch of pepper
    ½ cup uncooked potato cubes
        Or
    1 ounce soybeans, half-cooked
    ½ cup fresh green beans
    ½ cup sliced carrots
    Grated Parmesan cheese (optional)

Coat medium saucepan with no-stick vegetable spray and sauté onions until transparent, stirring to prevent sticking. Loosen tomato skins by spearing with fork and dipping them into boiling water. Cool slightly and slip skins off. Cut tomatoes into eighths and add, with salt, sweetener, and pepper, to onions. Simmer covered for 20 minutes. Add potato (or half-cooked soybeans), green beans, and carrots; cover, and cook 20 minutes longer until tender. Serve sprinkled with Parmesan cheese, if you like.

Serves 2 or 3.

SATURDAY DINNER

VEGETABLE CHEESE CASSEROLE

    2 cups diced, cooked, mixed vegetables, your choice of green beans (string beans, snap beans), corn kernels, carrots, peas, cauliflower, Brussels sprouts, bean sprouts, broccoli, celery, leeks, summer squash, etc. (May use canned mixed vegetables, drained.)

> 4 Chinese water chestnuts, sliced
> ½ cup low-fat pot or cottage cheese
> 1 ounce part skim cheese, such as Jarlsberg, grated
> Protein croutons (see recipe in this chapter), crumbled
> Minced parsley

Arrange cooked, drained vegetables in a small casserole coated with a no-stick vegetable spray. Spread pot or cottage cheese over vegetables, then sprinkle with grated cheese mixed with crumbled protein croutons. Heat uncovered in 400° oven 20 to 25 minutes, or until brown and bubbly. Sprinkle with parsley and serve with ½ cup of no-sugar applesauce mixed with 1 tablespoon raisins.

Serves 1.

SUNDAY DINNER

CHOW MEIN

A few, or all, of the following vegetables may be used. Adjust quantities accordingly.

> ¼ cup slivered almonds
> 1 onion, sliced thin
> 1 cup celery, sliced diagonally
> > choice of:
> ½ cup bamboo shoots (canned, drained)
> 1 small white turnip, sliced thin, cut into strips
> ½ green pepper, diced
> ⅛ teaspoon powdered ginger (or ¼ teaspoon minced ginger root)
> > choice of:
> 1 can water chestnuts, drained, sliced
> 1 cup bean sprouts
> 1 cup snow pea pods, fresh if available, or frozen, drained
> ½ pound mushrooms, sliced
> 1 tablespoon cornstarch
> 1 cup water
> 2 tablespoons no-sugar soy sauce

Strips of pimiento
1 cup cooked rice

Coat a large skillet or a wok with no-stick vegetable spray and sauté almonds, sprinkled with a little salt, until toasty. Remove almonds. Add sliced onion, cook 2 minutes, stirring. Add celery, bamboo shoots, turnip, pepper, and ginger, and cook 2 minutes, stirring. Add water chestnuts, bean sprouts, peapods, and mushrooms; again, cook 2 minutes, stirring. Mix cornstarch with water and add to vegetables with the soy sauce. Turn down heat and simmer all together 8 to 10 minutes. Add almonds and season to taste. Serve over hot rice and top with pimiento strips.

Serves 3 to 4.

PROTEIN CROUTONS

Cut 1 slice of protein bread into about 30 or more cubes. Coat a small skillet with no-stick vegetable spray and heat cubes over high flame, stirring until crispy and brown. Sprinkle with seasoned salt (or garlic salt, if preferred).

These may be used as croutons, or crumbled to breadcrumbs to enhance salads or other foods in any meal where 1 slice protein toast is indicated in the menu.

REPEAT THE DAILY MENUS for your second week on the Scarsdale Vegetarian Diet.

AFTER YOUR TWO WEEKS on the Scarsdale Vegetarian Diet, if you still want to lose more pounds to get down to your desired weight, go on to two weeks of Keep-Trim Eating, adapting to your regulations. Following that period, return to two more weeks on the Vegetarian Diet.

11
Scarsdale International Diet

For those who enjoy cooking, serving, and eating "something special," the Scarsdale International Diet, like the Gourmet Diet, provides something new and delightful in reducing—*the joy of eating epicurean meals day after day, and losing weight rapidly at the same time!*

Remember—*never overload your stomach.* You should lose an average of a pound a day on the Scarsdale International Diet, or up to 20 or more pounds in two weeks.

For any one day or meal, you may substitute the same day's eating or single meals (Monday for Monday, and so on) from the Scarsdale Medical Diet or any of the other Scarsdale Diets.

Here's how your International weeks shape up (repeat during the second week):

MONDAY: American Day
TUESDAY: Japanese Day
WEDNESDAY: French Day
THURSDAY: Italian Day
FRIDAY: Spanish Day
SATURDAY: Greek Day
SUNDAY: Hawaiian Day

Follow the basic rules precisely:

Scarsdale Diets Basic Rules
(Repeated here for your convenience.)

1. Eat exactly what is assigned. Don't substitute.
2. Don't drink any alcoholic beverages.
3. Between meals you eat only carrots and celery, but you may have as much as you wish.
4. The only beverages allowed are regular or decaffeinated coffee, black; tea; club soda (with

lemon, if desired); and diet sodas in all flavors. You may drink them as often as you wish.

5. Prepare all salads without oil, mayonnaise, or other rich dressings. Use only lemon and vinegar, or the vinaigrette or mustard dressing in Chapter 7, or dressings in Chapter 10.

6. Eat vegetables without butter, margarine, or other fat; lemon may be used.

7. All meat should be very lean; remove all visible fat before eating. Remove skin and fat from chicken and turkey before eating.

8. It is not necessary to eat everything listed, but don't substitute or add. Indicated combinations should be observed.

9. Never overload your stomach. When you feel full, *STOP!*

10. Don't stay on the Diet more than fourteen days.

KEEP THIS 14-DAY PROGRESS CHART OF YOUR WEIGHT LOSS:

	DAY 1	DAY 2	DAY 3	DAY 4	DAY 5	DAY 6	DAY 7
FIRST WEEK							
SECOND WEEK							

TOOK OFF ___ POUNDS

Scarsdale Diets: Substitute Lunch

If you wish, you may substitute the following lunch for any lunch, any day, on the Scarsdale International Diet:

½ cup low-fat pot cheese or cottage cheese, on lettuce

Sliced fruit, all you want, as exotic as you desire

1 tablespoon low-fat sour cream topping the fruit

6 halves of walnuts or pecans, chopped and mixed with the fruit, or sprinkled over the fruit

Coffee/tea—choice blends of your selection/ diet soda

After Your First Week

Repeat the daily menus here for your second week on the Scarsdale International Diet . . . or, if you like, you may substitute the week's menus of the basic Scarsdale Medical Diet, or one of the other Scarsdale Diets.

BREAKFAST EVERY DAY
½ grapefruit, or other fruit listed[1]
1 slice of protein bread, toasted
Coffee/tea (no sugar or cream or milk added, sugar substitute may be used)

YOUR CHOICE: In your daily Scarsdale International Diet menus, recipes for dishes marked with an asterisk* appear at the end of the entire week's menu listing.

If you prefer on any day not to use the listed recipe for lunch or dinner or both, simply substitute the lunch or dinner from the same day of the basic Scarsdale Medical Diet in Chapter 4. As an example, you may use the SMD Monday Lunch instead of the International Monday Lunch, and so on for every meal any day.

---

[1] *Choice of Fruit for Breakfast Every Day:* Grapefruit may be replaced any day by any of the following fruits in season:
   ½ cup diced fresh pineapple
   or ½ mango
   or ½ papaya
   or a generous slice of honeydew, casaba, or other available melon

MONDAY: AMERICAN DAY

Lunch:

Shrimp cocktail (4 medium shrimp, 2 tablespoons cocktail sauce)
*American Vegetable Salad
1 slice of protein bread, toasted
½ cantaloupe[1]
Coffee/tea

Dinner:

*Marinated Barbecue Steak
*Mushrooms and Cabbage in Wine
*Watermelon and Strawberries in Rosé Wine[1]
Coffee/tea

TUESDAY: JAPANESE DAY

Lunch:

*Japanese Vegetable Soup
*Tuna Shimi
*Mandarins Oki
Japanese tea/any tea/coffee

Dinner:

*Tori Shrimp and Chicken
*Bean Sprout and Green Pepper Salad
¼ cup plain boiled rice
*Fruits in a Mold
Japanese tea/any tea/coffee

[1] In all Scarsdale International Diet daily menus, any of the
fruits listed for breakfast may be substituted for the fruit
dessert specified on any lunch or dinner, if you prefer; however,
if no fruit dessert is specified, no fruit should be eaten.

WEDNESDAY: FRENCH DAY

Lunch:

>   One hard cooked egg
> *Marinated vegetables
>   No-sugar applesauce on apricot (fresh or water
>   packed)
>   Coffee/tea

Dinner:

> *Artichoke Provençale
> *Chicken à l'estragon
> *Celeri au jus
> *Poire glacée
>   Coffee/tea/demitasse

THURSDAY: ITALIAN DAY

Lunch:

> *Pickled Eggplant and Cheese Sticks
>   Salad greens, all you want, with vinegar and
>   lemon dressing
> *Peach with Raspberry Sauce
>   Coffee/tea/espresso

Dinner:

> *Baked Stuffed Mushrooms
> *Veal Napolitane
>   ¼ cup boiled white rice
> *Zucchini Stew
>   Coffee/tea/espresso

FRIDAY: SPANISH DAY

Lunch:

> *Eggs Gitano
>   Carrot sticks, 4 Spanish olives
>   1 slice of protein bread, toasted
>   Coffee/tea

Dinner:
> *Gazpacho soup
> *Zarzuela
>   ¼ cup cooked white rice (plain)
>   Sliced orange sprinkled with coconut
>   Coffee/tea

SATURDAY: GREEK DAY

Lunch:
> *Tomato Soup with Scallions
> *Feta Spinach Salad
>   1 slice protein bread, toasted
>   Coffee/tea

Dinner:
> *Lamb with Dolmas
> *Boiled Vegetables with lemon juice, vinegar and
>   chopped mint sauce (sauce may be used over
>   lamb, dolmas and vegetables)
> *Meringue Pear
>   Coffee/tea

SUNDAY: HAWAIIAN DAY

Lunch:
> *Clear Lemon Soup
> *Mixed salad of Pickled Vegetables
>   1 slice baked ham (1 ounce)
>   1 slice protein bread, toasted
>   Coffee/tea

Dinner:
> *Lomi Salmon
> *Bean Sprouts Salad
>   Broiled ½ zucchini flavored with garlic salt
> *Pineapple Surprise Aloha
>   Tea/coffee

Recipes

MONDAY LUNCH

AMERICAN VEGETABLE SALAD

    1 tablespoon plain gelatin
    ¼ cup clear chicken broth
    1 tablespoon chili sauce
    ½ cup cooked string beans, well drained
    ½ cup shredded raw carrots
    ½ cup diced raw celery
    1 ounce diced American cheese
    Salt and pepper
    ¼ head of lettuce
    1 tablespoon vinegar dressing

Dissolve gelatin in 1 tablespoon chicken broth. Heat remaining broth. Add gelatin and let cool 5 minutes. Mix with chili sauce. Add vegetables, cheese, salt and pepper. Pour into mold and chill until serving time. Unmold over lettuce and sprinkle with dressing. Serve at once.

    Serves 1.

MONDAY DINNER

MARINATED BARBECUE STEAK

    4 ounces T-Bone steak (weight without bone, all visible fat removed)

MARINADE FOR STEAK:

    Mix ½ cup beef broth with 1 tablespoon lemon juice, 1 tablespoon Teriyaki sauce, salt, pepper, and 1 crushed garlic clove or a dash of onion powder

Place steak in marinade. Let stand 2 or 3 hours, turning occasionally. Place on barbecue or under broiler. Cook to taste. Steak need not be drained before cooking.

    Serves 1.

MUSHROOMS AND CABBAGE IN WINE

 ½ cup fresh sliced mushrooms
 ½ cup sliced white cabbage, cooked in water
  and well drained
 1 tablespoon dry white wine
 Pinch of fresh or dry oregano
 Pinch of thyme
 Salt and pepper

Coat a skillet with no-stick vegetable spray. Cook mushrooms quickly, turning often. Add wine, herbs, seasonings. Mix, and add cabbage. Cover, heat about 10 minutes or until heated through. Serve at once.
 Serves 1.

WATERMELON AND STRAWBERRIES IN ROSÉ WINE

 1 cup diced watermelon
 ½ cup sliced strawberries
 1 teaspoon artificial sweetener
 2 ounces American Rosé wine
 1 teaspoon vanilla extract

Mix melon with strawberries and sweetener. Add vanilla and wine. Mix well, but gently. Chill before serving.
 Serves 1.

TUESDAY LUNCH

JAPANESE VEGETABLE SOUP

 1 cup instant chicken broth
 ¼ cup fresh mushrooms, sliced thin
 ¼ cup bamboo shoots, diced
 1 tablespoon diced celery
 1 teaspoon minced parsley leaves
 Salt and pepper
 Dash of garlic powder

Bring all ingredients just to a boil. Serve piping hot.
 Serves 1.

TUNA SHIMI

> 3½ ounces (½ can) tuna fish (packed in water, well drained)
> 1 tablespoon no-sugar soy sauce
> 2 teaspoons white horseradish sauce
> Dash of ground ginger or ⅛ teaspoon fresh ginger
> Salt and pepper
> 1½ cups spinach leaves
> 1 scallion sliced thin
> 1 tablespoon lemon juice
> 2 red radishes attractively carved

Mix soy sauce, horseradish, ginger, salt and pepper. Pour over tuna and mix lightly. Place on spinach leaves. Sprinkle with scallions and lemon juice. Add radishes. Chill until serving time.

Serves 1.

MANDARINS OKI

> ½ cup Mandarin oranges (packed in water, drained)
> 1 teaspoon artificial sweetener
> ⅛ teaspoon grated ginger
> Dash of cinnamon
> 1 teaspoon grated coconut

Arrange Mandarin segments in serving dish. Mix with flavorings and sprinkle with coconut. (This dessert may be lightly broiled and served hot, if preferred.)

Serves 1.

TUESDAY DINNER

TORI SHRIMP AND CHICKEN

> ½ cup raw shrimp (ready to cook)
> ½ chicken breast, no skin, no fat
> 1 cup water
> 2 tablespoons no-sugar soy sauce
> 1 teaspoon artificial sweetener
> ⅛ teaspoon five spices powder

    ½ cup sliced mushrooms
    ¼ cup sliced snow peas
    4 asparagus spears (frozen or canned or fresh)
    5 whole blanched almonds

Cut shrimps in halves, set aside. Dice chicken and set aside. Mix a little water with soy sauce, sweetener and spices. Cover mushrooms with ¼ cup hot water and set aside. Bring rest of water to a boil over very high heat. Add chicken. Cook 6 minutes, turning often. At the same time, coat a heavy pan with no-stick vegetable spray and add shrimps. Working rapidly, sauté shrimps until pink. Remove and keep warm. In the same pan, add snow peas, heat quickly. Remove and keep warm. Add asparagus, heat through, and remove pan from heat, leaving asparagus in the pan. Add mushrooms to the cooked chicken and its liquid and bring to a boil. Cook 3 minutes. With a slotted spoon, remove chicken and mushrooms, place in serving dish. Add shrimps and snow peas. Mix lightly. Sprinkle with some cooking juice (not too much, or the shrimps and snow peas will turn dark), garnish with asparagus and almonds. Serve at once.
    Serves 1.

BEAN SPROUT AND GREEN PEPPER SALAD

    1 cup well-washed and dried bean sprouts
    ½ cup shredded green peppers
    1 tablespoon vinegar
    Dash of grated fresh ginger
    Salt and pepper to taste

Mix bean sprouts and green peppers, add dressing, salt and pepper, ginger. Mix well. Chill until ready to serve.
    Serves 1.

FRUITS IN A MOLD

    ½ cup diced papaya
    2 fresh kumquats (if fresh kumquats are not available, use *one* preserved kumquat, with syrup washed off)
    3 lichee nuts, pitted, diced

1 tablespoon plain gelatin
1 teaspoon vanilla extract
1 teaspoon almond extract
¼ cup clear pineapple juice

Soften gelatin over hot water in a tablespoon of the pineapple juice. Add vanilla and almond extract and remaining pineapple juice. Set aside. Slice kumquats and mix with papaya and lichee nuts. Add gelatin mixture. Mix well. Pour into a small mold and chill until serving time. Unmold on serving dish, and if desired, garnish with mint leaves.

Serves 1.

WEDNESDAY LUNCH

MARINATED VEGETABLES

½ cup sliced zucchini, parboiled
½ cup string beans, cooked, well drained
½ cup green pepper, cut into strips
2 small cooked white onions
½ lemon cut into thin slices

MARINADE:

1 cup chicken broth
2 tablespoons dry white wine (optional)
2 tablespoons lemon juice
1 garlic clove, crushed
¼ cup chopped parsley
½ teaspoon dry thyme
1 teaspoon Worcestershire sauce
Salt and pepper

Stir together all the ingredients for marinade. Bring to a boil. Reduce temperature and simmer 30 minutes. Have vegetables ready and attractively arranged on a platter. Pour half of marinade on vegetables. Cover with aluminum foil or plastic wrap. Refrigerate until serving time. Taste; add more marinade if necessary. Garnish with lemon slices and serve. (The marinade will keep for a few days in the refrigerator.)

Serves 1.

WEDNESDAY DINNER

ARTICHOKE PROVENÇALE

     4 artichoke hearts (packed in water, well
        drained)
     ¼ cup green salad, any kind, shredded
     1 tablespoon chopped parsley
     1 teaspoon dry oregano
        Garlic powder to taste
        Salt and pepper
     ½ cup cooked peas (cooked in water, well
        drained)

Coat a small heavy-bottomed casserole with no-stick
vegetable spray. Add artichoke hearts, salad, and seasonings. Cover and simmer 10 minutes. Add peas and
heat. Serve piping hot, but do not overcook.
     Serves 1.

CHICKEN A L'ESTRAGON

     ½ medium chicken breast, skin removed, no
        bones
     ½ cup chicken broth
     2 tablespoons chopped fresh or dry tarragon
     1 tablespoon dry white wine mixed with 1 egg
        yolk
        Salt, pepper, a pinch of paprika

Preheat oven to 350°. Coat an ovenproof dish with
no-stick vegetable spray. Add ¼ cup chicken broth.
Place chicken in the broth and sprinkle with tarragon.
Season to taste. Wrap top and sides of dish with
aluminum foil and place in oven; bake 30 minutes.
Remove chicken, keep warm. Pour cooking juices into
a small pan and add remaining chicken broth. Bring
to a boil. Quickly add wine–egg yolk mixture, mixing
with a whisk until slightly thickened. Pour over chicken.
Garnish with more chopped tarragon if desired.
     Serves 1.

CELERI AU JUS
(May also be prepared with fennel)

>1 cup celery slices about 2 inches long (or 1 cup fennel slices)
>½ cup beef broth
>Salt and pepper
>1 tablespoon prepared Dijon mustard

Parboil celery slices in salted water for 10 minutes. Drain, keep warm. Heat beef broth with seasonings. Using a whisk, add a little hot broth to the mustard, mix well, and add remaining broth. Pour over celery. Serve warm.
   Serves 1.

POIRE GLACÉE

>1 small pear, peeled and cored
>¼ cup water
>2 ounces red wine
>1 tablespoon lemon juice
>1 teaspoon artificial sweetener
>1 teaspoon vanilla extract
>1 tablespoon plain gelatin

Bring water and wine to a boil in a small saucepan. Add lemon juice, artificial sweetener, and vanilla. Place pear in mixture. Cover and cook gently, turning occasionally, until pear in cooked through but still firm, about 25 minutes. Take pear out of juice with a slotted spoon and place in dessert dish. Dilute gelatin with a little water and add to hot wine mixture. Mix well, pour over pear. Cool until serving time.
   Serves 1.

THURSDAY LUNCH

PICKLED EGGPLANT AND CHEESE STICKS

>1 cup diced eggplant, with skin
>2 garlic cloves, mashed (or less, if preferred)
>1 small tomato peeled and seeded, diced
>1 small hot red pepper seeded, diced

    1 teaspoon fresh or dry oregano
    2 tablespoons beef broth
    1 tablespoon red wine vinegar
    Salt and pepper
    1 ounce Provolone cheese
    4 paper-thin slices of lemon

This recipe should be prepared the day before serving. Coat a small skillet liberally with no-stick vegetable spray. Add eggplant. Sauté at high heat, turning often, until lightly browned. Cover, cook 5 minutes at medium heat. Remove from pan and pour into a bowl. Mix all other ingredients except lemon. Pour over eggplant. Cover and let stand overnight in the refrigerator. At serving time, mix lightly and place on a plate. Cover with lemon slices. Slice cheese into sticks, arrange around eggplant. Serve.

Serves 1.

PEACH WITH RASPBERRY SAUCE

    2 peach halves, canned, packed in water (or fresh, if available)
    ½ cup raspberries, canned, packed in water (or fresh, if available)
    1 teaspoon vanilla extract
    ½ cup water
    Artificial sweetener to taste

Heat water, add raspberries. Cook 5 minutes. Add sweetener and vanilla extract. Mix in blender at high speed. Cool; pour over peaches. Chill until serving time.

Serves 1.

THURSDAY DINNER

BAKED STUFFED MUSHROOMS

    4 large mushrooms ready to cook, stems removed and chopped
    2 large chicken livers, chopped fine
    1 tablespoon chopped onion
    1 tablespoon chopped parsley

    1 teaspoon fennel seed
    ⅛ teaspoon garlic powder
    1 tablespoon low-fat cream cheese or low-fat
       Neufchâtel cheese
    ¼ cup chicken broth
    1 tablespoon lemon juice

Coat a heavy pan with no-stick vegetable spray. Add chicken livers, onions, and seasonings. Cook over low heat for 5 minutes, mixing gently. Add chopped mushroom stems. Cook 5 minutes more. Remove from heat and mix with low-fat cream cheese or Neufchâtel cheese. Stuff each mushroom cap with mixture. Put caps in a baking dish, sprinkle with lemon juice. Cover with aluminum foil and bake at 350° for 30 minutes. Remove covering and heat 5 minutes longer; transfer to serving dish and pour broth around mushrooms.
    Serves 1.

VEAL NAPOLITANE

    ¼ pound veal scallopini
    Salt, pepper, garlic powder to taste
    1 garlic clove, mashed (or less, to your taste)
    1 tablespoon very lean chopped ham
    1 tablespoon chopped parsley
    ¼ cup dry wine (red or white)
    1 teaspoon capers
    1 small artichoke heart (canned in water or
       frozen)
    ¼ cup tomato juice

Place meat between sheets of wax paper and pound well. Sprinkle with seasonings. Coat a small heavy skillet with no-stick vegetable spray, add veal. Fry quickly for 2 minutes. Remove from pan. Add to pan garlic, ham, and parsley. Bring to boil. Add tomato juice, adjust for seasonings. Bring to a second boil. Reduce heat and simmer 5 minutes more. Add capers. Pour over meat, mixing well. Place artichoke heart on top of the veal just before serving.
    Serves 1.

ZUCCHINI STEW

 ½ small zucchini, sliced thin
 1 tablespoon beef broth
 1 tablespoon tomato juice
 1 teaspoon dry thyme, mixed with
 1 teaspoon dry oregano
 1 teaspoon chopped onion
 Salt and pepper

Pour beef broth and tomato juice into the bottom of a small casserole. Add zucchini slices, herbs, onion, and seasonings. Cook at low heat for 30 minutes. Serve hot.

Serves 1.

FRIDAY LUNCH

EGGS GITANO

 2 hard cooked eggs
 1 tablespoon chopped onion
 1 clove garlic, crushed
 ½ tomato, peeled, seeded, chopped
 ¼ cup green pepper
 Salt and pepper to taste
 1 tablespoon chopped parsley
 1 tablespoon beef broth
 ⅛ teaspoon artificial sweetener
 ¼ cup green beans
 3 asparagus spears (cooked or canned)

Have all ingredients ready since this recipe will be cooked in a few minutes.

Coat a skillet with no-stick vegetable spray. Add onion, garlic, tomato, and green pepper. Cook at medium heat, stirring, until onions are transparent. Add seasonings, parsley, beef broth, sweetener. Mix. Carefully add green beans and egg quarters. Cook a few minutes more or until eggs are heated through. Turn out on a serving dish. Garnish with asparagus spears. Serve at once.

Serves 1.

FRIDAY DINNER

GAZPACHO SOUP
    ¼ cup diced peeled cucumber
    ¼ cup finely chopped green peppers
    ¼ cup diced, seeded tomato
    ¼ cup diced celery
    1 tablespoon chopped onion
    ½ cup tomato juice
    1 teaspoon Worcestershire sauce
    1 tablespoon lemon juice
    Salt, pepper, a pinch of cayenne pepper

Mix all the vegetables in the tomato juice. Add lemon juice and seasonings. Chill very well until time to serve.
    Serves 1.

ZARZUELA
    4 clams (whole Little Necks)
    6 medium shrimps, cleaned and ready to cook
    3 ounces crab meat (chunks)
    ½ tomato, seeded, diced
    1 tablespoon chopped onion
    1 clove garlic, crushed
    ⅛ teaspoon saffron
    1 pinch of cayenne pepper
    Salt, pepper
    ¼ cup dry white wine mixed with
    ¼ cup water
    ¼ cup minced parsley

Coat a heavy medium casserole with no-stick vegetable spray. Add onions and tomato. Cook quickly, turning with a wooden spoon. Add saffron and garlic; mix. Add clams, cover casserole, and cook 5 minutes. Add wine, shrimps, crab meat, seasonings. Cover. Cook at high heat until shrimps are pink and clams open. Sprinkle with parsley, stirring food quickly. Serve at once.
    Serves 1.

SATURDAY LUNCH

TOMATO SOUP WITH SCALLIONS
½ cup beef broth
½ cup plain tomato juice
2 teaspoons chopped onion
Pinch of ground cloves
2 tablespoons diced celery
½ teaspoon dry dill
Salt, pepper, a pinch of cumin
⅛ cup chopped green scallions (or chives)

Bring beef broth and tomato juice to a boil. Add onion, celery, and seasonings. Cook at low heat 10 minutes. Add dill, simmer 5 minutes. Add scallions (or chives, if scallions unavailable) and serve at once.
Serves 1.

FETA SPINACH SALAD
2 cups spinach (raw)
¼ cup cooked white rice
1 hard cooked egg, cut in quarters
1 small sweet red pimiento, cut into ¼-inch pieces
1 small cucumber, diced
1½ ounces crumbled feta cheese
2 tablespoons vinegar dressing
2 Greek olives

Mix spinach with rice, egg quarters, pimiento, cucumber, feta cheese. Add dressing. Mix lightly. Garnish with Greek olives. Serve at once.
Serves 1.

SATURDAY DINNER

LAMB WITH DOLMAS
4 ounces very lean roast lamb, no juice
3 SMALL DOLMAS:

    3 medium size vine leaves (in brine, well
      drained)
    ¼ cup cooked white rice
    1 tablespoon chopped onion
    ⅛ teaspoon cumin
    Salt and pepper
    ¼ cup chicken broth

Place a teaspoonful of rice, mixed with onion and
seasonings, in the middle of a vine leaf. Fold; starting
at base, fold over. Fold in sides, rolling tightly until
rice mixture is well enclosed. Repeat with other leaves.
Pour broth into the bottom of a small heavy casserole.
Arrange stuffed vine leaves side by side and cover tightly. Cook 30 minutes at low heat.

    Following the same proportions, you may cook about
20 at the same time. (Dolmas will keep in their cooking
juice in the refrigerator for about 2 weeks.)
    Serves 1.

BOILED VEGETABLES WITH LEMON-MINT SAUCE

    ½ cup string beans
    ½ zucchini, sliced (or ½ cup sliced)
    ½ cup dandelion greens, or ½ cup spinach
    Salt, pepper
    A pinch of dill

Cook string beans 8 minutes in boiling salted water.
Add remaining vegetables and cook gently until greens
are just tender. Drain well. Serve hot with sauce made
of lemon juice, vinegar, and chopped mint, which may
also be spooned over lamb and dolmas.
    Serves 1.

MERINGUE PEAR

    1 medium pear, peeled and cored but left whole
    1 teaspoon artificial sweetener
    1 teaspoon almond extract
    1 egg white

Preheat oven to 375°. Cook pear in water until tender
but firm. Drain. Coat the bottom of a small baking

dish with no-stick vegetable spray. Place pear in the center. Beat egg white until frothy, add sweetener and almond extract. Continue beating until stiff but not dry. Using metal spoon, cover the fruit with the meringue. Brown in oven for about 10 minutes. Remove from oven. Serve at room temperature or chilled.

Serves 1.

SUNDAY LUNCH

CLEAR LEMON SOUP
    1 packet chicken broth
    1 cup water
    1 tablespoon lemon juice
    3 tablespoons finely chopped spinach
    1 teaspoon lemon peel
    Salt, pepper
Add dry broth to water and bring to a boil. Add lemon juice, seasonings. Cook 5 minutes. Add spinach and lemon peel. Heat 5 minutes longer. Serve piping hot.

Serves 1.

MIXED SALAD OF PICKLED VEGETABLES
    2 carrots cut into strips
    ⅓ cup bamboo shoots cut into strips
    ½ cup cucumber cut into strips
    ¾ cup shredded white cabbage
    ½ medium tart apple
    1 teaspoon ground ginger
    1 teaspoon artificial sweetener
    1 teaspoon coarse salt, pepper
    ¼ cup white vinegar
    1 scallion, minced
    1 garlic clove, minced
    2 tablespoons water
Mix spices with vinegar and water. Add scallion and garlic. Pour over mixed vegetables. Mix well. Let stand in the refrigerator until serving time. Should be prepared the day before if possible.

Serves 1.

SUNDAY DINNER

LOMI SALMON

    4 ounces fresh salmon (boned and skinned)
    2 tablespoons chopped onion
    1 tablespoon minced scallions, green part in-
       cluded (or chives, if preferred)
    ½ teaspoon fresh or ground ginger
    Salt and pepper
    ¼ teaspoon Tabasco sauce
    ¼ cup lime juice
    ½ cup chopped, peeled, seeded tomato
    4 thin slices lemon

Coat the bottom of a heavy baking dish with no-stick
vegetable spray. Place salmon in the dish and cover
with onion and scallion. Season. Add Tabasco and
lime juice. Cover dish with aluminum foil and bake in
350° oven for 25 minutes. If the liquid evaporates,
add some hot water. Remove aluminum foil. Add
tomatoes and cook 5 minutes longer. Serve with lemon
slices.
   Serves 1.

BEAN SPROUTS SALAD

    ½ cup well-washed and drained fresh bean
       sprouts
    1 tablespoon vinegar
    ⅛ teaspoon minced fresh ginger
    Salt
    Dash of Worcestershire sauce

Mix all ingredients. Serve very cold.
   Serves 1.

PINEAPPLE SURPRISE ALOHA

    ½ small pineapple
    ¼ cup diced papaya
    1 tablespoon kumquat peel (candied)
    1 tablespoon rum (optional)
    1 teaspoon artificial sweetener

Carve out inside of pineapple half to form a cavity. Chop the pineapple meat. Mix with papaya, kumquat peel, rum, and sweetener. Pile mixture into pineapple cavity. Cover with plastic wrap. Refrigerate until 20 minutes before serving time.

Serves 1.

REPEAT THE DAILY MENUS for your second week on the Scarsdale International Diet.

If you want to lose still more pounds after two weeks on the Scarsdale International Diet, go on to two weeks of Keep-Trim Eating. Following that, return to two more weeks on any of the Scarsdale Diets of your choice.

12
Be a Scarsdale Loser and a Lifetime Winner

The tips here are reminders and suggestions for living the fat-free life. It has been said that the way to reduce could be stated in two words: "NO thyself." That's true to a point, but alone it doesn't work. The specific Scarsdale Diets do.

• *Chew! Chew! Chew!* I can't overemphasize that. It's a big help in dieting not to rush your eating. And you'll enjoy every bite more.

• *Instead of high-calorie snacks,* keep a bowl of carrot sticks, celery stalks, zucchini and cucumber slices in water in the refrigerator at all times. Having these items handy can make all the difference. Sugarless beverages, including tea and coffee without sugar, cream, or milk, also help to assuage hunger in those who need such help. They can be taken at any time.

• *Build a mountain* when you make a salad. Pile up plenty of lettuce, tomatoes, radishes, celery, carrots, green peppers. Add lemon juice or one of the Scarsdale Diet dressings. You'll have loads to eat, with practically no fat and few calories.

• *Avoid second helpings.* Adding "a little more" can add a lot more pounds eventually. Second helpings become a destructive habit. Learn to say "No, thanks" to a persuasive hostess and to yourself.

• *A gourmet chef's fat-trimming tip:* You can often cut more fat off raw and cold cooked meat with a sharp scissors than with a knife. You have better control, and can cut closer.

• *Keep your eye on your weight-loss goal,* instead of griping about giving up rich, fatty, sweet foods. A researcher asked women what three words they like most to hear. Instead of the expected answer, "I love you" —the consensus was: "You've lost weight."

• *Check the printed calorie counts* on so-called "low-calorie" and "dietetic" foods. Some "dietetic" cookies were found to be higher in calories than the regular type! Vital calorie savings do exist in some "low-calorie" foods, but make sure.

• *Keep in mind dry wines* to add flavor in cooking. The alcohol burns off, but food taste is enhanced.

• *Order fish broiled "dry" in restaurants,* with just a little lemon or wine used for moisture. Good fish is more delicate and much lower in calories and fat without butter, margarine, or oil.

• *Cup up your food*—it goes further and is more satisfying. Instead of gobbling a whole peeled banana in a minute, cut it into slices on cottage cheese—makes a satisfying serving rather than a hasty snack.

• *Be wary at coffee breaks.* If a neighbor invites you over for cookies and coffee, enjoy the coffee but learn to skip the cookies ("I'm on the Scarsdale Diet"). You'll avoid the fats and calories, and a good neighbor will understand.

• *Speak up when being served*—before the hostess piles your plate, it's perfectly all right to say, "Please go easy—I feel better when I eat less, and I don't want to leave that good food on my plate."

• *Fill your sugar bowl with sugar substitute,* and carry sugar substitute packets with you. If you formerly drank four cups of coffee a day and used two teaspoonfuls of sugar per cup, you are saving 144 calories a day by using sugar substitute.

• *Ignore the tray of rolls* while you're waiting for your food to arrive in a restaurant. A hard roll spread with a thick pat of butter can add up to nearly 300 extra calories!

• *Enjoy the fresh, piquant taste of vegetables* rather than disguising their special flavors with butter, margarine, or rich sauces. For instance, six stalks of cooked asparagus seasoned with lemon juice amount only to about 20 calories, but with melted butter sauce they can soar up to 300 calories and lots of *fat* where there was no fat at all!

• *Be wary when traveling—never overeat.* Stuffing yourself invites and aggravates digestion problems. When butter, sauces, gravies, custards, pastries, mayonnaise, and other foods containing eggs or milk are exposed too long, bacteria multiply. In some areas where refrigeration is faulty, food may be contaminated. If you're not sure that raw vegetables and fruits are thoroughly washed in "safe" water, it's better to avoid them (instead, order fruits you can peel, such as bananas, oranges, apples). In some places, drink only bottled water. If you're not accustomed to spicy "hot" foods, skip them in order to avoid discomfort, and worse.

• *Refrigerator tip from a Scarsdale Dieter:* "With the whole family on the Diet, I taped this sign on the refrigerator door: 'Keep America Beautiful—Stick to the Scarsdale Diet. There are no forbidden foods in this house.'"

• *Avoid rich dressings on restaurant salads.* Order salad plain, with lemon wedges and vinegar "on the side."

• *Use your imagination in preparing meals.* All the delicious Scarsdale Diet recipes use permitted ingredients. Make your own tasty combinations of the foods designated for lunch and dinner. For example, for Thursday lunch, you can combine the eggs, stewed tomatoes, crumbled protein toast, and a little cottage cheese in an omelet "masterpiece."

• *Carry your Scarsdale Diet lunch* in a thermos or other containers if you like eating at work or play. You'll be joining the nationwide Scarsdale Keep-Trim crowd.

• *When you feel satisfied, STOP!* I can't stress enough that overloading your stomach is a health hazard, aside from piling on overweight. I read somewhere that obesity is the penalty for exceeding the *"feed limit."*

• *Don't let anyone convince you* that gourmet cooking requires rich, high-fat ingredients. The Scarsdale Gourmet Diet proves the opposite. Two of the world's great chefs, France's Paul Bocuse and Michel Guérard, brought to French cooking, *Time* Magazine reported, "A new emphasis on freshness and simplicity." Bocuse commented, "Cuisine and dieting are no longer contradictions." Two of the rules of their cuisine are: "Hold the butter! Dam the cream!"

• *Make sure your frying pan* is a non-stick skillet or use no-stick vegetable spray rather than oil or butter to keep foods from sticking. For moistening, you can also sauté in a little broth or dry wine.

• *Be proud that you're taking off weight.* You have a lot of company if my mail and telephone are any indication. When eating out, it's a cinch to stick to your Scarsdale Diet in a restaurant. It's acceptable everywhere now to order soda-with-lime instead of a highball; a permitted dish like broiled chicken, steak, roast lamb, or a chop, instead of something rich and creamy even if it's the *chef's spécialité*. "Maybe next time— right now I'm on the Scarsdale Diet."

• *"A snapshot helped me,"* a Scarsdale Dieter reported. "I had one of those instant photos taken of me in a bathing suit the day before I started dieting. I looked forward to having a similar picture taken two weeks later. It was worth waiting for!"

• *"Feeding a cold"* is another dieting "myth," just an excuse some overweights give for eating forbidden foods. Actually a cold or fever usually diminishes the appetite. Stuffing in rich food definitely is not good medical practice.

• *Watch out when you're watching TV.* Beware of the usual TV-watchers' snacks—potato chips, pretzels, peanuts, beer. Instead, keep handy a bowl of the inevitable but fat-free carrots, celery stalks, broccoli, cauliflower buds, green pepper strips, cherry tomatoes; diet sodas and lime or lemon wedges. A wife-and-husband dieting team said they took up knitting and macramé "to keep our hands busy and out of the snack bowl while watching TV with the kids."

• *Keep moving, keep walking.* A favorite recommendation of a fine physician was: "Don't lie down if you can sit . . . don't sit if you can stand . . . don't stand if you can walk." Walking briskly not only uses up some calories, it can help you enjoy life more.

• *Put food in perspective in your life.* A tall man in his mid-twenties reduced from 260 to 185 pounds. He credits not only an excellent diet but also a change in mental perspective: "I finally realized that high-fat, high-carbohydrate foods kept me fat and sick. My face was always broken out. My gut swelled out like a barrel. My back ached, causing constant pain. I suddenly said to myself, 'Why am I suffering—for gobs of ice cream, masses of sweets and fat that I stuff in my mouth?' I started dieting, took up swimming in the community pool for an hour nightly. My complexion and back troubles are gone. My reaction to rich foods now is *Yccchh!* And the reaction women have to the new me is Wow!"

• *Be aware of everything you eat.* Overweight people often stuff themselves with food without realizing it. A very heavy acquaintance sat at a bar chatting while waiting to be seated in a crowded restaurant, a huge bowl of peanuts at his elbow. In a little while his wife pointed out that he had emptied the bowl. He blurted, "My God, I don't remember eating the peanuts. I didn't even enjoy them!" Be aware—and beware.

• *Use instant broth—a real help.* Mix up a packet of instant chicken, meat, fish, or vegetable broth in water in seconds. In cooking and in skillets, it often eliminates the need for butter, margarine, oil, other fats. If you wish to reduce the saltiness, use double the amount of water in package directions, add a splash of flavoring such as Worcestershire sauce.

• *Stop thinking of desserts* in terms of something rich, such as ice cream, cakes, puddings, pies. Think *fruit*— an attractive fruit cup without sugar, a wedge of melon, a half grapefruit, sliced orange, or an apple, peach, pear, plum, or sliced banana and other fruits in no-sugar gelatin. They all satisfy a "sweet tooth" once you break the high-fat, high-sugar habit.

• *Learn to add calorie-free flavor in cooking.* Flavor with herbs, spices, seasonings (dozens are listed in the

Medical Appendix), dry wines, shallots, mushrooms, vegetables, and greens. James Beard, discussing "life without butter," after he was forced to diet, suggested: "You're forced to be creative . . . Last night, for example, I wanted to have a chop . . . I put the chop in a bed of tarragon surrounded by shallots and a very small amount of white wine . . . The meal was delicious."

• *Diet with a companion.* It helps to compare daily Scarsdale weight-chart scorecards with family, friends, others who go on the Diet at the same time. Members of a local tennis club bring their Scarsdale Diet brown bags to the courts, enjoy eating lunch together and comparing SMD scorecards. One observed, "As the pounds go down, our spirits go up."

• *Stay at your desired weight,* neither above nor below. A few newly trim individuals become so thrilled about their slim figures that they go to extremes and keep taking off pounds long after they should stabilize.

• *Reward yourself* at the end of your two-week Scarsdale Diet, not only by switching to Keep-Trim Eating, or going back to normal eating if you are down to your desired weight goal—but also by treating yourself to something you want—a new book, a new tie or scarf, theater tickets—something you will enjoy that you have kept in mind as an end-of-diet treat. Meanwhile, you'll be lots lighter and you will have learned good new eating habits.

• *Don't look back.* Some overweights maintain that since they've always failed on diets in the past, there's no hope for the future. Take this tip from Confucius: *"What is past, one cannot amend . . . For the future, one can always provide."*

• *We have tried in every possible way to make your Scarsdale Lifetime program simple, effective, and enjoyable.* For example, you won't find a better fish recipe anywhere than Cold Poached Fish Natalia with Mustard Sauce Henri, both on the Gourmet Diet. With such recipes, you and your guests will find it hard to believe this is low-fat, low-carbohydrate, low-calorie dining.

• *Check special diet information throughout.* If you

have any special medical problems you and your doctor may find helpful information in the Medical Appendix. It includes among other things:

- Foods Permitted on Sodium-Restricted Diets
- Food Prohibited Where Sodium Restriction Is Indicated
- Seasonings, Spices, Herbs Permitted on Sodium-Restricted Diets
- Foods High in Potassium
- Allergy Elimination Diet
- Limited High-Carbohydrate Foods for Diabetics
- Typical Rice Diet
- High-Cholesterol Foods to Avoid
- High-Carbohydrate Foods to Avoid
- High-Fiber, High-Bulk, Good Elimination Guidelines

13
Answers to More
Questions You May Have
After Being on
the Scarsdale Diet

For all of you who are on, or about to go on the Scarsdale Medical Diet, this chapter is important and useful. Don't skip over it. An intelligent, well-informed dieter, like an intelligent, well-informed patient, is always the best kind.

Most of your questions about details of the Scarsdale Medical Diet have been answered in Chapter 5. The answers here cover not only the Scarsdale diets specifically, and how they can work best for you, but also dieting and lifetime good health in general. They can help you further to get down to your desired weight now, and to learn and follow good eating habits—to keep trim from now on.

Most of these questions would never have occurred to me. Each is one I have been asked, in most cases not once but many times. I put the first half dozen at the top of the list because I consider them particularly important.

Q. *Lunch on your Wednesday SMD menu calls for tuna fish. Is it all right if I cut up the carrots and celery and mix them in with the tuna fish?*

A. A woman called from Canada to ask this question, and I have had similar ones from Cleveland, Washington, and Scarsdale. It sounds simplistic but is isn't. It springs from a misinterpretation of certain newspaper articles about the Scarsdale Medical Diet which led some people to believe that any slight alteration would destroy the "chemistry" of the Diet.

The Scarsdale Medical Diet contains a carefully selected, sound, effective combination of proteins, fats, and carbohydrates. Its unique quality lies in the fact that it is basically simple to follow; you are not hungry while dieting; and *you lose weight.*

But the Diet is *not* alchemy—mix two parts zucchini, one part heart of toad, a dash of tuna fish—and presto, dietary gold! It *is* a good combination of healthful foods, a "just right" combination, if you will, but it is not a chemical formula. Putting the carrots and celery in with the tuna fish is of no consequence.

Q. *All my life I've been told that the one perfect food is milk. Why isn't there milk on the Scarsdale Medical Diet?*

A. This question has been asked of me by some doctors as well as by patients and other dieters. Milk *is* a very good food, but there is a certain amount of mythology about how much of it we actually need, or how much of it is good for us. Many nutritionists, among them Dr. Mark Hagsted, of Harvard, have concluded that our bodies do not need the high calcium intake we once thought they did.

Most important, there are some fairly recent and convincing studies showing that many people lose the ability to digest lactose well before adolescence. For them, the undigested lactose can cause considerable intestinal discomfort as it ferments in the colon. I was interested to learn that U.S. Marine Corps cadets during their extremely strenuous eleven-week boot-camp training are not permitted to drink milk.

Dr. John Farquhar, member of the Stanford Heart Disease Prevention Program, wrote recently in his book, *The American Way of Life:* "As large percentages of people cannot properly digest lactose, it plainly makes no sense to promote the indiscriminate quaffing of milk. Even those people fortunate enough to process the critical enzyme would do well to cut down their intake of whole-milk dairy products. Unless people limit their dairy intake to nonfat milk or low-fat cottage cheese, they consume far greater quantities of butter-fat than is healthy."

When you finish your two weeks on the Scarsdale Medical Diet, by all means go back to skim or low-fat milk if you enjoy it. But two weeks without it offer no problems or hazards; in fact, depending on what your milk-drinking habits were before, the change may well be good for you.

Q. *What can I do for an overweight teenager?*
A. I'm always saddened to see young people who are overweight. It means they probably have been taught, or have been permitted, to indulge in bad eating habits. If carrots and celery and fresh fruit are the snack that is readily available to young children, they will learn to enjoy these instead of large quantities of sweet junk food. Start now, while you are on the Scarsdale Medical Diet yourself, to take a careful look at the eating habits you are helping to teach your children.

Q. *Being fat just runs in my family. We're all overweight. How can the Scarsdale Medical Diet do anything for me?*
A. Overweight "running in a family" is one of the most insidious dietary myths. It must be put out of your mind before a long-term diet program will really work for you. There *are rare cases* of genetic obesity about which little is yet known. I emphasize "rare." If everyone in a family is overweight, chances are everyone in that family *overeats*.

Obesity is largely preventable. The prescription for curing it can be found right here in the Scarsdale Medical Diet and the Keep-Trim Program. Unfortunately, it is a little harder for those who have spent a lifetime developing the habit of overeating to develop new and wiser diet behavior patterns to follow the rest of their lives.

That's the bad news. But I like to remind my patients of the good news, too. Fortunately for all of us, once excess fat has accumulated, it can be reduced safely and fairly quickly with proper diet. When calorie intake is reduced, the body utilizes *excess fat* instead of muscle, hair, bone, or other body essentials. The body automatically establishes priorities for you, hangs on to the essentials, and gets rid of what you can safely spare.

Q. *How did the name* Scarsdale Medical Diet *come about?*

A. As I mentioned earlier, I have practiced medicine in Scarsdale, New York, for over 40 years. My offices are in the Scarsdale Medical Center, which I built 19 years ago. The name came from the Scarsdale location—that's its only significance. The Scarsdale Medical Diet by any other name would be just as effective.

Q. *Will giving up* salt *help me lose weight?*

A. Cutting down on salt won't help you lose body weight since it contains no calories. But excess salt intake can increase fluid retention. Some people should be on salt-restricted diets (see material on Congestive Heart Failure in the Medical Appendix).

Q. *What do you advise basically to help prevent health problems, and to stay healthy?*

A. My answer will be confined to what teenagers and adults should do. I suggest that three physical examinations be done between the ages of thirteen and thirty, three in the fourth decade of life, and after fifty, I believe an annual physical examination is desirable.

This should include:

1. A careful history.
2. A physical examination.
3. A baseline chest x-ray, electrocardiogram, urine, complete blood count and complete blood chemical analyses.

It would be beyond the scope of this book to describe how each of the above contributes to diagnosis and treatment. Suffice to say, physicians frequently wish they had previous baselines for comparison. Early metabolic defects are frequently identified (such as obesity, high cholesterol, or elevated triglycerides) at a time when they can be treated most effectively. Hypertension, diabetes, and a host of other abnormalities are occasionally discovered. Your physician gets to know you and your family. This helps him and benefits you in many ways; that is, there may be a genetic or metabolic "weakness" in the family which would routinely come to his attention.

Q. *I was born with a "sweet tooth" and can't give up sweets; what do you suggest?*
A. That's another popular myth. An orthodontist friend calls it "mother's myth." Have a diet soda when you want a sweet. Keep carrots and celery handy instead of sweet snacks.

Q. *Should I avoid beer when trying to lose weight?*
A. Yes, while you're dieting—stick to the basic Scarsdale Medical Diet Rules. When you are back to regular eating and on Keep-Trim Eating, keep in mind that beer is high in calories, so regulate your intake. As you'll find in the C-P-F-C Charts in Chapter 14, "low-calorie" beer *is* much lower in calories—under 100 calories per twelve-ounce can, compared with about 150 calories for regular beer.

Q. *Do I have to eat my slice of protein bread on the Diet whole, or can I crumble it on the other foods if I wish?*
A. Use the bread in any form you wish. For example, note the delicious recipe for Protein Croutons at the end of the Vegetarian Diet.

Q. *I feel terribly guilty—at breakfast with the family I let go and ate three sweet coffee rolls and six slices of buttered toast; what should I do, starve for a few days?*

A. We all have our failings. Fortunately, your dereliction is not catastrophic. Start over again, determine to succeed.

Q. *I developed "hunger pains" and had to break the diet; how I can prevent the pains and yet lose weight?*

A. It is not uncommon to experience hunger pains when you change old poor habits for a more disciplined regime. It may take a few days to overcome this symptom, but eventually your metabolism will accept the better approach. In the meantime, if you are too uncomfortable, have a piece of fruit in season—pear, peach, or some other.

Q. *I had to entertain a client at a business lunch, had to go along with a martini and dessert, and gained a few pounds. How can I prevent this?*

A. Your client is probably a sensible, intelligent person. All you have to do is to urge her to have what she wants and explain why you are having a soda and more simple fare.

Q. *My best friend is a gourmet cook who piles food on my plate; we eat there often and I can't bear to insult her by not eating; what can I do?*

A. We all let down occasionally. I would suggest that you explain to your friend that you would like to have small portions because of the goal you have in mind. Many years ago I took a trip through France with a well-known publisher who was recovering from an illness. One of the conditions I laid down for him was that he was to *taste everything and eat almost nothing.* My advice to you is eat everything but very little of it.

Q. *I slimmed down beautifully on your Diet, but now I'm going through menopause and am compensating by eating; is there anything I can do?*

A. The menopause can be a trying period for some women. There is no need for you to gain weight because of the menopause—watch your diet.

Q. *Ever since I started taking birth control pills, my appetite has boomed and so has my weight; how can I control my cravings?*

A. It is most unlikely that birth control pills have any appreciable effect on your appetite. You may be using them unconsciously as an excuse.

Q. *Whenever I diet, I get cranky, and my husband says, "I like you better fat than cranky"; have you any suggestions?*

A. You should be able to diet without getting cranky. Your husband, I am sure, would like to have you attractive, lean, and pleasant. The diets we have listed should help you.

Q. *After a few days of dieting, I start to feel draggy and dizzy; is it my imagination or what?*

A. Occasionally, not very frequently, people have complained of the symptoms you describe. They will gradually subside. In the meantime, don't hesitate to take a piece of fruit, which will help to elevate your blood sugar level and allay your discomfort.

O. *I had to feed my cold and dry throat so I ate soothing ice cream and hard candies; what are my alternatives?*

A. I would suggest that instead you try tea with lemon and mint, sweetened with sugar substitute.

Q. *I diet and lose weight, a pound a day, Monday through Thursday, then put it all back on and more over our social weekend; any solution?*

A. Your dilemma is a frequent one. If you find it impossible to follow the Scarsdale Medical Diet on weekends I would suggest that you stick to the Keep-Trim Eating guidelines on those days.

Q. *I lost a lot of weight on your diet and my mother said, "You're so thin, you'll get sick." How can I answer her?*

A. Your mother has a common maternal failing. Many mothers equate love with feeding their young. If you are now at your normal weight she may not be used to seeing you this way.

Q. *I've gained a lot since delivering my baby, and maybe my metabolism or something has changed because I keep falling off the diet; have I changed inside somehow?*

A. It is entirely possible, but not common, for a person's metabolism to change after delivery. You should see your physician to make certain of whether or not this has happened to you.

Q. *I've lost 18 pounds on the Diet in two weeks, still have 20 pounds more to lose, but I feel weak and listless; what do you recommend?*

A. Moderate exercise such as walking, swimming, tennis, or other sports, will help you overcome the weakness and listlessness you are experiencing.

Q. *An intelligent friend told me that I stay very fat because I want to avoid sex by being less attractive to men; can that be true?*

A. It is entirely possible that your friend is right. You, however, should be able to analyze the situation and determine if this is in fact so.

Q. *When I see on the scale first thing in the morning that I've lost a pound or two, I eat more that day; how can I control myself?*

A. I personally weigh myself every day to see how much I can cheat. I have no objection to your going off the Keep-Trim guidelines as long as you are down to a proper weight. Set a goal that you feel you must reach before you start cheating.

Q. *I've lost 20 pounds, 15 more to go, but the skin on my face seems to be sagging; will facial exercises or anything help me?*

A. The sagging skin that one occasionally sees after a large weight loss will in practically every instance shrink within a reasonable period of time.

Q. *In the second week of my diet, after losing over a pound a day, and sticking to the diet, I hit a plateau the past three days; why is that?*

A. This happens with a small percentage of dieters, and is overcome by staying on the Diet, observing the SMD Basic Rules precisely. Check yourself to make absolutely sure that you are not "cheating," eating and snacking foods prohibited on the Diet, or overloading your stomach with excessive portions—the primary reasons for a "plateau."

Be patient and persistent—stay on the Diet for the full two weeks, then go on Keep-Trim Eating for two weeks, then back to one of the Scarsdale Diets. Continue with the Two-On–Two-Off program until you are down to your desired weight.

Q. *I take diuretic pills for high blood pressure, and my doctor told me to drink orange juice daily; won't that spoil my diet?*

A. The loss of potassium one occasionally sees as a result of taking diuretic pills is easily overcome by many high potassium foods that we have listed. It is perfectly safe and proper for you to take a little orange juice if really needed.

Q. *I gave up smoking, and find myself snacking all the time, can't stop myself; should I start smoking again?*

A. Don't start smoking again. I would suggest that you use a false cigarette as a pacifier until you overcome the habit of having something in your mouth. Also, munching on carrots and celery may help.

Q. *I should stop smoking, but isn't it true that everybody who stops smoking gains a lot of weight?*

A. No, it is not true that everyone who stops smoking gains weight. If you find that you are nibbling nervously, have the snacks I recommend at hand to overcome that habit.

Q. *I'm in the kitchen a lot cooking for my large family many rich dishes; how can I keep myself from tasting and spoiling my diet?*

A. *Taste* everything but *eat* nothing, as I advised the publisher I mentioned earlier.

Q. *My only relief from business pressures is through rich food; what can I do about it?*

A. Try the Scarsdale Gourmet or International Diets list to see if that will help you. There is no reason why you can't have exotic, tasty food. It just doesn't have to be high in calories.

Q. *When members of my family leave food on their plates, I can't resist not letting good things go to waste, so I finish their leftovers; any advice to help me?*

A. The compulsion to completely clean a plate is a common one. It is really a very bad habit that takes tremendous will power to overcome. I would urge everyone *always* to leave something on the plate.

Q. *I stay on the diet during the day quite easily, but at dinner my wife puts a rich homemade dessert in front of me and I can't resist; how can I tell her "no" without offending her?*

A. It is no simple matter to prepare a rich homemade dessert. Try to explain to your wife that you would prefer to have her make one of the low-calorie, tasty desserts we have listed in the various Scarsdale Diets (after your two weeks on the Scarsdale Medical Diet).

Q. *After a week of dieting and losing weight, I notice little spots and cracks on my tongue—are they due to dieting?*

A. It is quite possible that cracks and spots on your tongue are the result of an allergy to one of the foods you are eating. Check this out. Also, are you sure those "little spots and cracks" weren't there before your dieting, and that you're not just using them as an excuse?

Q. *At least once a day I feel that if I don't have something with real sugar, I'll collapse; can you suggest substitutes to satisfy me?*

A. It is quite possible that you have conditioned your body to the need for sugar. I am sure that if you eat some fruit in season—which contains a form of sugar called fructose—this unpleasant symptom will subside.

Q. *I spent three weeks convalescing from a bad illness, ate a lot, and gained weight—is it safe for me to go on your diet to reduce?*

A. It is not only safe for you to go back on your diet—it is most desirable!

Q. *I was doing well on your diet but I became constipated, and to overcome it ate a lot of bulky food that caused me to gain weight; how can I handle that problem?*

A. There is no need for you to gain weight because of the roughage you need to overcome constipation. See the list recommended for this condition in the Medical Appendix. As one gets older, the need for a daily cathartic is not unusual. I have patients who have taken a senna preparation every day for over 30 years, with very satisfactory results.

Q. *I'm 30 pounds overweight according to weight tables but I feel terrific—so why should I reduce?*

A. Thirty pounds of excess weight is a tremendous hazard. There is no doubt in my mind that you will feel more "terrific" when you get down to a proper weight.

Q. *My husband warns that losing weight will weaken me, and with a houseful of kids, I must stay strong; is he right?*

A. Obesity never made it easy to take care of a household and a bunch of screaming youngsters. You will be stronger lean and mean.

Q. *I wanted to diet but my boss said, "Don't do it, everybody loves a fat man"—do you agree?*
A. I would be very wary of your boss's advice. I hope his judgment is better in business matters. It is the lean, strong, well-tailored person who is admired today.

Q. *I started the diet when I weighed 140 pounds, aiming for my goal of 120 pounds. I'm delighted that I'm down to 125, but after four days back on the Scarsdale Medical Diet, I've been stabilized at 124 pounds. A friend says this is due to "fluid retention." What should I do to get down to my goal?*
A. It is quite possible that you have some fluid retention, which is not uncommon. Check with your physician who will probably order a diuretic to help resolve this question immediately. It is likely that you will lose the additional excess weight either by a diuretic, or by staying on the Scarsdale Medical Diet for another week.

Q. *I'm 46 years old, and some of my friends are jogging and running daily for exercise. Is it okay for me to join them?*
A. I strongly advise against jogging at your age. It is not unusual for people over 40 years of age to develop knee and other foot and leg problems as the result of this activity. Furthermore, you would have to jog for one hour to lose 600 calories. It is much easier to lose weight by proper dieting. Extensive research has indicated that approximately 300 calories a day should be expended through some type of physical activity. Walking, swimming, golf, and tennis are good choices.

Q. *I'm very heavy, finally losing weight happily. I sleep about 10 hours a night, and nap every afternoon. It's been suggested that I'll slim down faster if I sleep less. Do you agree?*

A. I do not have enough information about your age, occupation, and other matters, to answer your question intelligently. I frequently recommend an afternoon nap for very busy executives over 60 years old. Ten hours of sleep is quite a bit but there are people who need that much. The amount of sleep required is a very individual matter, but there's no question that when you are up and active, you use up more calories than when asleep.

Q. *I'm losing weight on your good diet but not as fast as I'd like. I think I may have a faulty metabolism. Could that be preventing the speedy weight loss that my friends are enjoying on your diet?*

A. It is entirely possible that you have a metabolic or endocrine disorder (affects only about 5 percent of people). Your family physician can very easily help you resolve this question.

Q. *I'm losing pounds and inches on your great diet. Would I lose inches faster by adding strenuous exercising daily?*

A. Strenuous exercise is fine for the young. As mentioned, I don't recommend it for anybody 40 years of age or over unless they are in good shape and accustomed to that type of activity. Also, I believe it is important to avoid exercises that build huge muscle masses unless you are engaged in an occupation that requires unusual muscular ability. Enjoy your exercises, but pursue those sports that give you satisfaction.

Q. *Have you personally ever had a weight problem, and if so, how did you lick it?*

A. I have never had a serious weight problem. But I know that I can easily put on weight if I don't follow the Keep-Trim Eating guidelines. I weigh myself every day to see how much I can cheat. I enjoy the Scarsdale Optional Lunch practically every day.

Q. *On my second round on the Scarsdale Medical Diet, when I substitute the Gourmet, Money-Saver, Vegetarian, and International Diets, can I alternate days one to the other if I wish?*
A. Yes, but always substitute the same day—for example, Vegetarian Monday for Gourmet Monday, and so on.

Q. *I've never been able to eat much for breakfast; may I have my breakfast slice of protein toast instead as a snack between meals, or at another meal?*
A. Perfectly all right.

Q. *I lost 21 pounds on your Diet, but also after having very bad psoriasis for 16 years, it cleared up on the Diet; is this usual?*
A. People have reported skin problems clearing up as they get rid of a lot of excess pounds, but it may or may not be due to the Diet.

Q. *I was a heavy baby, and I've read that people accumulate "fat cells" and can't reduce; does the Scarsdale Medical Diet overcome that problem?*
A. Whether or not they have excess "fat cells," many obese people have succeeded in taking off their overweight on the Diet.

Q. *My husband says he's "naturally fat" and therefore can't lose weight; is that true?*
A. I question anyone being "naturally fat" since I've seen so many people who have been fat all their lives finally trim down on the Scarsdale Diets. If your husband has a metabolic or other problem causing his overweight, his doctor should be able to help control that.

Q. *Do you approve eating high-fiber foods?*

A. High-fiber foods are fine but some are high in calories; they possess no magical properties. See "High-Fiber High-Bulk Eating Guidelines" in connection with "Constipation" in the Medical Appendix.

Q. *My adolescent youngster is 14, and quite overweight; is it all right for her to go on the Scarsdale Medical Diet?*

A. I prefer that youngsters diet under the personal supervision of their doctors.

Q. *My whole family was always overweight as I grew up; how can I help my children avoid following that pattern?*

A. By setting a good example. Prepare sensible meals. Keep trim and lean. Don't insist that plates be cleaned.

Q. *If I lose 20 pounds in two weeks on the Scarsdale Medical Diet, won't that leave me weak and tired?*

A. No, just the opposite. Dropping 20 pounds of overweight increases energy and endurance, like putting down a 20-pound bag of groceries that you've been carrying a long way.

Q. *I've heard that sex exertion uses up more calories than anything else; is that true?*

A. Enjoy yourself, but if you're overweight, don't expect to get thin through sex. Sex is fine, but afterward if you eat a small apple, all the calories are back!

Q. *I lost my excess pounds on the Scarsdale Medical Diet, but I've just returned from a wonderful month's vacation where I gained 12 pounds; what do I do now?*

A. I'm glad you enjoyed your vacation. Now go right back on the Scarsdale Medical Diet.

Q. *Can you recommend a diet to help prevent cancer?*

A. In brief: There is increasing medical opinion that various types of cancers may be associated with poor dietary habits. A National Cancer Institute scientist stated that close to 100,000 American cancer deaths, 30–40 percent of the annual total, could be prevented by changes in smoking, drinking, and eating habits . . . and that 5,000 breast cancer deaths annually, one out of six, could be prevented if American women would eat less saturated fats.

It is the consensus of many cancer specialists that a low-fat, low-carbohydrate, low-cholesterol eating pattern may lower a person's risk of cancer. That's the kind of eating recommended throughout this book, but with no claims about inhibiting cancer. Intensive research by the National Cancer Institute and many others offer hope of clarifying links between cancer, diet and specific eating guidelines. But right now, I don't know of any valid cancer-prevention diet.

Q. *Is it more difficult to lose weight after having a baby?*

A. Not necessarily, but some women find it so. You can trim down by sticking to it, as indicated in this letter from a lady I don't know: "After I had my baby a year ago, I was appalled that my weight was 150 pounds . . . I had never weighed more than 120 pounds. I tried other diets, was constantly hungry, and after eight months was down only to 135 pounds. I discovered the Scarsdale Medical Diet. In two weeks I was down to 120 pounds—and I'm staying there!"

Q. *I'm too* skinny; *how can I GAIN WEIGHT?*

A. This is a problem for an estimated five million people in the United States. It's not easy for the underweight person who usually doesn't care for food. Here are suggested guidelines for two heavy-eating weeks to add 10 to 15 pounds, *not* recommended as a lifetime eating pattern.

Your attitude must be that you will "force" yourself to eat more, just as a determined overweight person refrains from eating forbidden foods during the SMD two-week period. First have a medical checkup to make sure that your underweight isn't due to specific physical or emotional problems—*this is a must!*

Your daily program for the two weeks: Make it a ritual to *sit down* to three sizeable meals a day, as many courses as you can manage. Take your time, try to *enjoy* every mouthful. Add high-calorie snacks such as sweets, potato chips, nuts, malteds, throughout the day and evening. *Socialize!* You'll eat more in the company of others.

Check the C-P-F-C Charts of Foods in Chapter 14, and make *high-calorie choices* in every category: Vegetables—limas rather than green beans, creamed corn instead of carrots. Canned fruits in heavy syrup, dates, figs, dried apricots. Beverages—thick milk shakes, malteds, whole milk, chocolate milk, ice cream sodas, heavy cream and sugar in hot chocolate, coffee, tea. Thick lentil and bean-frankfurter soups.

Don't trim fat off meat or skin off poultry. Add rich sauces, gravies. Eat buttered bread, biscuits, pies, cakes, French toast, pancakes, waffles. Load cereals with cream and sugar. Macaroni products, rice, with rich sauces. Ice cream sundaes with fudge and butterscotch sauces; thick puddings topped with whipped cream and nuts. Whole milk and heavy cream cheeses.

If you smoke, stop.

Weigh yourself first thing each morning to make sure you are gaining; keep a daily weight scorecard (as on SMD). At the end of the two weeks, you should have had a change in eating habits to help you eat more and maintain your weight gain. Keep tabs on the scale daily thereafter.

Q. *Is it all right for me to go back on the Scarsdale Medical Diet at any time through the years ahead if I get overweight?*

A. By all means (but always check with your doctor to be sure you haven't undergone a health change). I've had patients return to the Diet when needed for almost 20 years, with happy results.

14
Special Information
That Will Help You

As you pursue your goal of lifetime leanness you will find some of the tables, charts, and special information in this chapter of help.

Activity and Exercise Calorie-Usage Chart

The following table indicates *approximately* how many calories (energy units) are used by the body during *a half-hour of basic activity*. Because of the many individual differences, figures cannot be precise, but these can serve as general guidelines.

It has been determined that, to keep fit, the average individual should expend at least 300 calories a day in some activity such as walking, golf, or tennis. It is extremely difficult to lose significant weight through exercise. A half-hour of energetic bicycling, for instance, uses up 200–280 calories, which you put right back on by eating an iced cupcake.

ACTIVITY/EXERCISE	120-POUND WOMAN (*calories*)	160-POUND MAN (*calories*)
Badminton	180–220	220–260
Baseball	160–200	200–240
Basketball	300–400	400–600
Bicycling moderately	100–120	120–140
Bicycling energetically	200–230	280–320
Bowling	80–120	100–140
Canoeing	100–150	130–180
Carpentry, workbench	120–140	140–180
Climbing stairs	130–160	160–190
Cooking, active	60–90	80–110
Dancing moderately	100–130	130–170
Dancing energetically, disco	200–400	250–500
Dishwashing, by hand	60–90	80–110

ACTIVITY/EXERCISE	120-POUND WOMAN (*calories*)	160-POUND MAN (*calories*)
Dressing, undressing	30–50	35–60
Driving auto	50–60	60–75
Dusting energetically	80–100	80–110
Exercising moderately	140–170	180–220
Exercising energetically	200–250	250–350
Football	250–300	300–400
Gardening, active	120–140	140–180
Golf, no cart	100–140	130–170
Golf, with cart	70–90	80–110
Handball	200–350	300–400
Hockey, field, ice	250–350	300–400
Horseback riding	140–160	160–200
Housework, active	80–130	110–160
Ironing	60–80	70–90
Jogging, light	200–250	250–300
Lacrosse	250–350	350–400
Lying, sitting, at rest	15–20	20–25
Office work, active	70–130	90–150
Painting walls, furniture	130–150	150–180
Piano playing	80–130	100–150
Polishing furniture, auto	80–120	90–150
Reading	15–20	20–25
Rowing vigorously	300–400	400–500
Running	300–400	400–500
Sawing wood	250–300	300–400
Sewing	25–30	30–35
Singing	35–40	40–60
Skating energetically	200–300	250–350
Skiing energetically	200–300	250–350
Soccer	250–350	350–400
Squash	180–240	250–400
Standing, relaxed	20–25	25–30
Sweeping floor	80–100	90–110
Swimming steadily	200–300	300–400
Table tennis	150–180	200–250
Tennis, amateur	180–220	250–280
Typing	80–100	90–110
Violin playing	70–100	90–130
Volleyball	180–220	220–280
Walking moderately	80–100	90–120
Walking energetically	140–160	160–180
Writing	25–80	30–100

If you engage in activities which are not listed in the preceding, you can figure out the calorie usage approximately by checking the numbers of a comparable activity. How energetically you participate personally has a lot to do with how many calories you use up.

Following is a chart that shows you the number of calories you can consume daily to maintain your weight at the normal level for your height and sex (naturally, your frame and the amount of exercise you get will also play a part in how much you can consume without gaining).

DESIRED WEIGHT AND MATCHING CALORIE MAINTENANCE CHART
(Based on height; no clothing.)

	WOMEN		MEN	
HEIGHT	Weight in pounds	Daily calories	Weight in pounds	Daily calories
4'10"	90 98	1080–1170	95–105	1235–1365
4'11"	93–102	1115–1225	98–108	1275–1405
5'	95–105	1140–1260	100–111	1300–1445
5'1"	97–108	1165–1295	105–117	1365–1520
5'2"	100–111	1200–1335	110–123	1430–1560
5'3"	105–118	1250–1415	115–128	1495–1665
5'4"	110–123	1320–1475	120–133	1560–1730
5'5"	112–126	1345–1515	125–138	1625–1795
5'6"	117–130	1405–1560	130–143	1690–1860
5'7"	120–134	1440–1610	133–148	1730–1925
5'8"	125–139	1500–1670	137–153	1780–1990
5'9"	130–144	1560–1730	143–159	1860–2065
5'10"	135–149	1620–1790	148–164	1925–2130
5'11"	140–154	1680–1850	152–168	1975–2185
6'	144–158	1730–1895	155–171	2015–2225
6'1"			163–179	2120–2325
6'2"			167–183	2170–2380
6'3"			170–188	2210–2445
6'4"			172–195	2235–2535
6'5"			178–198	2315–2575
6'6"			185–206	2405–2680

Write your desired weight goal here: _____ pounds
Write your daily calorie allowance here: _____
calories

Composition of Foods Calories—Protein—Fat—Carbohydrates

The tables that follow are a dependable general guide to what is in most of the foods used by many people from time to time. Since foods vary in many ways, the counts are approximate rather than absolutely precise in every instance. The figures are derived primarily from U.S. Department of Agriculture charts, rounded for clarity rather than carried to the ultimate decimal.

You don't count calories on the Scarsdale Medical Diet or the follow-up programs, because you follow the simple menus (which run roughly under 1,000 calories a day). But with these tables, those of you who are interested or curious can check the calories of most foods and beverages. Your best guide is your daily weight on the scale.

COMPOSITION OF FOODS

FOODS: PORTION	CALORIES	PROTEIN (grams)	FAT (grams)	CARBO-HYDRATES (grams)
MEATS AND POULTRY				
Bacon, crisp, drained, thin sliced: 2 slices	95	5	8	1
Bacon, Canadian, crisp, drained, trimmed: 1 oz.	79	8	5	trace
Beef, trimmed, cooked:				
Braised, simmered, pot-roasted				
Lean and fat:				
3½ oz.	286	27	19	0
Lean only: 3½ oz.	196	31	7	0
Hamburger, broiled				
Regular market ground:				
3½ oz.	286	24.5	20	0
Ground lean: 3½ oz.	216	27	11.5	0
Rib, or other relatively fat roast, oven-cooked without liquid:				
Lean and fat: 3½ oz.	455	19	42	0

FOODS: PORTION	CALORIES	PROTEIN (grams)	FAT (grams)	CARBO-HYDRATES (grams)
MEATS AND POULTRY				
Beef (continued)				
Lean only: 3½ oz.	233	27	14	0
Round, or other relatively lean cut:				
Lean and fat: 3½ oz.	256	27	16	0
Lean only: 3½ oz.	182	29	5.5	0
Steak, broiled: relatively fat, such as sirloin				
Lean and fat: 3½ oz.	385	23	31.5	0
Lean only: 3½ oz.	201	31.5	7	0
Porterhouse:				
57% lean, 43% fat:				
3½ oz.	465	19.5	42	0
Separable lean: 3½ oz.	224	30	10.5	0
T-Bone				
56% lean, 44% fat:				
3½ oz.	473	19.5	43	0
Separable lean: 3½ oz.	223	30	10	0
Club steak:				
58% lean, 42% fat:				
3½ oz.	454	20.5	40.5	0
Separable lean: 3½ oz.	244	29.5	13	0
Beef, corned beef				
Cooked, medium fat:				
3½ oz.	372	23	30	0
Canned lean: 3½ oz.	185	26	8	0
Beef, dried or chipped: 2 oz.	372	23	30	0
Beef liver, fried: 3½ oz.	229	26	10.5	5.5
Cooked without fat (or raw): 3½ oz.	140	20	4	5.5
Beef Tongue				
Cooked, braised: 3½ oz.	244	21.5	17	0
Canned or pickled:				
3½ oz.	267	19	20	trace
Chicken cooked:				
Broilers:				
Flesh and skin, broiled, without bone: 3½ oz.	216	28	11	0
Light meat, without skin:				
3½ oz.	166	31.5	3.5	0
Dark meat, without skin:				
3½ oz.	176	28	6	0
Roasters:				
Flesh and skin, roasted:				
3½ oz.	248	27	14.5	0
Flesh only, roasted:				
3½ oz.	183	29.5	6	0
Canned, boneless: 3½ oz.	170	25	7	0

FOODS: PORTION	CALORIES	PROTEIN (grams)	FAT (grams)	CARBO-HYDRATES (grams)
MEATS AND POULTRY				
Livers, simmered: 3½ oz.	165	26.5	4.5	3
Lamb:				
Leg (choice grade): total edible, cooked, roasted (83% lean, 17% fat): 3½ oz.	279	25	19	0
Separable lean, roasted: 3½ oz.	186	28.5	7	0
Loin (choice grade): total edible, broiled chops (72% lean, 25% fat): 3½ oz.	293	16.5	25	0
Separable lean, broiled chops: 3½ oz.	188	28	7.5	0
Shoulder (choice grade): cooked, roasted (74% lean, 26% fat): 3½ oz.	338	21.5	27	0
Separable lean: 3½ oz.	205	27	10	0
Pork, fresh: Composite of trimmed, lean cuts: ham, loin, shoulder, and spareribs:				
Medium fat class, cooked, roasted (77% lean, 23% fat): 3½ oz.	373	22.5	30.5	0
Separable lean: 3½ oz.	236	28	13	0
Chop, thick, with bone: 3½ oz.	260	16	21	0
Chop, lean only: 1.7 oz.	130	15	7	0
Roast, oven-cooked, no liquid added				
Lean and fat: 3 oz.	310	21	24	0
Lean only: 2.4 oz.	175	20	10	0
Pork cured:				
Ham, medium-fat:				
Cooked, roasted, (84% lean, 16% fat): 3½ oz.	289	21	22	0
Separable lean: 3½ oz.	187	25	9	0
Canned 3½ oz.	287	18	12	1
Picnic:				
Cooked, roasted (82% lean, 18% fat): 3½ oz.	323	22.5	25	0
Separable lean: 3½ oz.	211	28.5	10	0
Rabbit, cooked, stewed: 3½ oz.	216	29	10	0

FOODS: PORTION	CALORIES	PROTEIN (grams)	FAT (grams)	CARBO-HYDRATES (grams)
MEATS AND POULTRY				
Sausage, cold cuts and luncheon meats:				
Bologna (average):				
3½ oz.	277	13.5	23	3.5
Braunschweiger: 3½ oz.	319	15	27.5	2.5
Cervelat (soft) :3½ oz.	307	18.5	24.5	1.5
Country style sausage:				
3½ oz.	345	15	31	0
Deviled ham, canned:				
3½ oz.	351	14	32.5	0
Frankfurters, cooked:				
3½ oz.	304	12.5	27	1.5
Liverwurst, smoked:				
3½ oz.	319	15	27.5	2.5
Luncheon meat:				
Boiled ham: 3½ oz.	234	19	17	0
Pork Sausage, links or bulk, cooked:				
3½ oz.	476	18	44	trace
Salami, dry: 3½ oz.	450	24	38	1
Sweetbreads:				
Beef, cooked: 3½ oz.	320	26	23	0
Calf, cooked, 3½ oz.	168	32.5	3	0
Lamb, cooked: 3½ oz.	175	28	6	0
Turkey:				
Total edible, cooked, roasted: 3½ oz.	263	27	16.5	0
Flesh and skin, roasted:				
3½ oz.	223	32	9.5	0
Flesh only, cooked, roasted: 3½ oz.	190	31.5	6	0
Light meat, cooked, roasted: 3½ oz.	176	33	4	0
Dark meat, cooked, roasted: 3½ oz.	203	30	8.5	0
Veal:				
Average cut, medium fat, trimmed, roasted (86% lean, 14% fat): 3½ oz.	216	28.5	10.5	0
Cutlet, broiled without bone: 3 oz.	185	23	9	4
FISH AND SHELLFISH				
Anchovy, canned: 3 fillet	21	2.5	1	trace
Bass, black sea:				
Poached, or broiled or baked without fat:				
3½ oz.	93	19	1	0
FISH AND SHELLFISH				
Bass, striped, raw: 3½ oz.	105	19	2.5	0

FOODS: PORTION	CALORIES	PROTEIN (grams)	FAT (grams)	CARBO-HYDRATES (grams)
Bluefish, raw: 3½ oz.	117	20.5	3.5	0
Clams, raw, meat only:				
3½ oz.	76	12.5	1.5	2
Canned, drained: 3½ oz.	98	16	2.5	2
Juice: 3½ oz.	19	2.5	trace	2
Cod, cooked or broiled:				
3½ oz.	170	28.5	5.5	0
Dried, salted: 3½ oz.	130	29	1	0
Crab, Dungeness, rock and King, cooked,				
steamed: 3½ oz.	93	17.5	2	.5
Fish sticks, frozen,				
cooked: 3½ oz.	176	16.5	9	6.5
Flounder, raw: 3½ oz.	79	16.5	1	0
Haddock, raw: 3½ oz.	79	18.5	trace	0
Halibut, Atlantic & Pacific, cooked, broiled:				
3½ oz.	171	25	7	0
Herring, raw:				
Atlantic: 3½ oz.	176	17.5	11.5	0
Pacific: 3½ oz.	98	17.5	2.5	0
canned, tomato sauce:				
3½ oz.	176	16	10.5	3.5
pickled: 3½ oz.	223	20.5	15	0
Salted or brined: 3½ oz.	218	19	15	0
Kippered: 3½ oz.	211	22	13	0
Lobster, northern, canned or cooked: 3½ oz.	95	19	1.5	.5
Mackerel, canned: 3½ oz.	183	19.5	11	0
Salted: 3½ oz.	305	18.5	25	0
Smoked: 3½ oz.	219	24	13	0
Mussels, meat only: 3½ oz.	95	14.5	2	3.5
Ocean perch (redfish):				
3½ oz.	88	18	1	0
Octopus, raw: 3½ oz.	73	15.5	11	0
Oysters, raw:				
Eastern: 3½ oz.	66	8.5	2	3.5
Western: 3½ oz.	91	10.5	2	6.5
Oysters, fried: 3½ oz.	239	8.5	14	18.5
Pike, raw: 3½ oz.	90	19	1	0
Pompano, raw: 3½ oz.	166	19	9.5	0
Red Snapper (and gray) raw: 3½ oz.	93	20	1	0
Salmon, Atlantic, raw:				
3½ oz..	217	22.5	13.5	0
Canned, solids and liquids:				
3½ oz.	203	21.5	12	0
Chinook (King), raw:				
3½ oz.	222	19	15.5	0
Canned, solids and liquids:				
3½ oz.	210	19.5	14	0

FOODS: PORTION	CALORIES	PROTEIN (grams)	FAT (grams)	CARBO-HYDRATES (grams)
FISH AND SHELLFISH				
Salmon (continued)				
Coho, canned, solids and liquids: 3½ oz.	153	21	7	0
Cooked broiled or baked: 3½ oz.	182	27	7.5	0
Smoked: 3½ oz.	176	21.5	9.5	0
Scallops, bay and sea cooked, steamed: 3½ oz.	112	23	1.5	—
Frozen, breaded, fried, reheated: 3½ oz.	194	18	8.5	10.5
Seabass, white, raw: 3½ oz.	96	21.5	.5	0
Shad, raw: 3½ oz.	170	18.5	10	0
Shrimp, canned, meat only: 3½ oz.	116	24	1	1
French fried: 3½ oz.	225	20.5	11	10
Sole, raw (also flounder, sandcrabs): 3½ oz.	79	16.5	1	0
Swordfish, raw: 3½ oz.	118	19	4	0
Trout, brook, raw: 3½ oz.	101	19	2	0
Rainbow or steelhead raw: 3½ oz.	195	21.5	11.5	0
Tuna, canned in oil:				
Solids and liquid: 3½ oz.	288	24	20.5	0
Drained solids: 3½ oz.	197	29	8	0
Canned in water: 3½ oz.	127	28	1	0
Weakfish, raw: 3½ oz.	121	16.5	5.5	0
Whitefish, lake, raw: 3½ oz.	155	19	8	0
Smoked: 3½ oz.	155	20	7.5	0
FRUITS AND FRUIT PRODUCTS				
Apples, raw, 1 medium (2½" diam.)	70	trace	trace	18
Applesauce, fresh: 1 cup	125	trace	0	32
Applesauce, canned:				
Sweetened: 1 cup	185	trace	trace	47
Unsweetened: 1 cup	100	trace	trace	25
Apricots, raw, 12 per lb.: 3	60	1	trace	14
canned in heavy syrup: 1 cup	218	1.5	trace	53
Dried, uncooked: 40 halves, small: 1 cup	390	7.5	1	89
Cooked, unsweetened, fruit and liquid: 1 cup	260	5	1	62
Nectar: 1 cup	143	1	trace	34
Banana, raw, about 3 per lb.: 1	130	2	trace	30.5
Blackberries, raw: 1 cup	85	2	1	17
Blueberries, raw: 1 cup	89	1	1	19

FOODS: PORTION	CALORIES	PROTEIN (grams)	FAT (grams)	CARBO-HYDRATES (grams)
FRUITS AND FRUIT PRODUCTS				
Cantaloupe, raw, ½ melon, 5″ diam.	40	1	trace	9
Cherries				
raw, sour: 1 cup	116	2	0.5	25
raw, sweet: 1 cup	140	2.5	.5	32
Cranberries				
canned sauce, sweetened, strained: 1 cup	400	trace	.5	99
Juice, cocktail, canned: 1 cup	130	trace	trace	32
Cranberry-Orange relish, raw: 3½ oz.	178	trace	trace	45
Dates, dried, pitted: 1				
medium	27	trace	trace	6.5
1 cup	525	4	1	120
Figs, dried, 2″ x 1″: 1 fig	60	1	trace	15
Fruit cocktail, canned, in heavy syrup (with liquid): 1 cup	195	1	trace	47
Grapefruit, raw, med., 4¼″ diam.: ½ fruit	50	1	trace	12
raw sections: 1 cup	75	1	trace	18
canned, water pack: 1 cup	70	1	trace	17
juice, fresh: 1 cup	95	1	trace	23
canned:				
unsweetened: 1 cup	100	1	trace	24
sweetened: 1 cup	130	1	trace	32
frozen concentrate, water added: 1 cup	115	1	trace	28
Grapes, raw, green:				
seedless: 1 cup	102	4	trace	27
other (approx.): 1 cup	100	1	trace	26
Grape juice, bottled: 1 cup	165	1	trace	42
Lemons, raw, 2⅛″ diam.:				
1 lemon juice:	20	1	trace	6
1 tbs.	5	trace	trace	1
Lemonade concentrate, water added: 1 cup	110	trace	trace	28
Lime juice, fresh: 1 tbs.	4	trace	trace	1
Limeade concentrate, water added: 1 cup	103	trace	trace	26
Mandarin oranges, canned, with syrup: 1 cup	125	1	.5	30
Mango, raw, edible part: ½ lb.	155	1.5	1	35
dried or sliced: ½ cup: 2½ oz.	53	.5	.3	12
Nectarine, raw: 1 med.	50	.5	trace	12

FOODS: PORTION	CALORIES	PROTEIN (grams)	FAT (grams)	CARBO-HYDRATES (grams)
FRUITS AND FRUIT PRODUCTS				
Orange, raw:				
Navel, California, 2⅘" diam: 1 orange	60	2	trace	13
others, 3" diam.: 1 orange	70	1	trace	17
Orange juice, fresh:				
California: 1 cup	120	2	1	26
Florida: 1 cup	100	1	trace	23
Canned, unsweetened: 1 cup	120	2	trace	28
frozen concentrate, water added: 1 cup	110	2	trace	26
Papaya, raw, ½" cubes:				
1 cup	71	1	trace	17
1 large	156	2	trace	38
Peaches, raw, medium: 2" diam. (4 per lb.):				
1 peach	33	.5	trace	8
sliced: 1 cup	65	1	trace	16
Canned in heavy syrup, 2 halves, 2 tbs. syrup	96	trace	trace	24
Water pack: 1 cup	75	1	trace	19
Peach nectar, canned: 1 cup	124	trace	trace	31
Pears, raw (3" x 2½" diam.): 1 pear	100	1	1	24
canned in heavy syrup, halves or slices: 1 cup	200	1	trace	50
Canned, water packed: 1 cup	80	trace	trace	20
Pear Nectar, canned: 1 cup	130	1	trace	33
Persimmons, Japanese or Kaki, raw, 2½" diam.: 1	80	1	trace	20
Pineapple				
raw, diced: 1 cup	75	1	trace	19
Canned in syrup, crushed: 1 cup	205	1	trace	50
Sliced (slices and juice): 2 sm.	95	trace	trace	25
Canned, packed in own syrup: 3½ oz.	58	trace	trace	15
Pineapple juice, canned: 1 cup	120	1	trace	31
Plums (not prunes): raw, 2" diam., about 2 oz.: 1 plum	30	trace	trace	7
canned in syrup: 3 plums, 2 tbs. juice	90	trace	trace	23

FOODS: PORTION	CALORIES	PROTEIN (grams)	FAT (grams)	CARBO-HYDRATES (grams)
FRUITS AND FRUIT PRODUCTS				
Prunes (continued)				
Prunes, dried:				
Medium, 50 or 60 per lb.: 4	80	1	trace	19
Cooked, unsweetened, 17–18 prunes and ⅓ cup liquid: 1 cup	330	3	1	80
Prune juice, canned: 1 cup	185	1	trace	42
Raisins, dried: 1 cup	462	4	trace	111
Raspberries, red, raw: 1 cup	70	1	.5	16
Frozen, sweetened: 1 cup	196	1.5	trace	47
Rhubarb, cooked, sugar added: 1 cup	385	1	trace	98
Strawberries, raw: 1 cup	55	1	1	11
Frozen, sliced, sweetened: 1 cup	247	1	trace	60
Tangerines, raw 2½" diam., about 4 per lb.: 1	40	1	trace	10
Tangerine juice, canned: unsweetened: 1 cup	105	1	trace	25
Frozen, water added: 1 cup	115	1	trace	27
Watermelon, raw:				
4" x 8" wedge	240	4.5	2	52
balls or cubes: 1 cup	56	1	trace	12
VEGETABLES				
Artichoke, cooked: 3½ oz.	44	3	trace	10
Artichoke hearts, frozen: 3 oz.	22	1	trace	4
Asparagus, med. spear, canned:	3	trace	trace	.5
6 spears	20	2	trace	3
Avocado, large: ½	180	2	16.5	6
Bamboo shoots, raw: 3½ oz.	27	2.5	trace	5
Bean sprouts:				
cooked (mung beans): 1 cup	28	3	trace	5
raw: 1 cup	26	3	trace	4
Bean sprouts (soy bean): 1 cup	50	7	1	5
Beans, green, cooked: 1 cup	25	2	trace	6
wax, cooked: 1 cup	22	1.5	trace	4.5
lima (green), cooked: 1 cup	197	13	1	35
dry lima, cooked: 1 cup	265	15.5	1	49
red kidney, cooked: 1 cup	234	15	1	42.5

FOODS: PORTION	CALORIES	PROTEIN (grams)	FAT (grams)	CARBO-HYDRATES (grams)
VEGETABLES (continued)				
Beets, diced: 1 cup	70	2	trace	16
Broccoli: 1 cup	50	5	trace	8
Cabbage, raw, shredded:				
1 cup	25	1	trace	5
cooked: 1 cup	40	2	trace	9
Cabbage (Chinese cabbage):				
raw 1" pieces: 1 cup	15	1	trace	2
cooked: 1 cup	25	2	1	4
Carrots, 5½", raw: 1 cup	20	1	trace	5
diced: 1 cup	45	1	1	9
Cauliflower, cooked,				
flowerbuds: 1 cup	30	3	trace	6
Celery, 8" stalk, raw:	5	1	trace	1
diced, cooked: 1 cup	20	1	trace	4
Corn, cooked, 5" ear:	65	2	1	16
canned, with liquid: 1 cup	170	5	1	41
Cucumber, 1 med. raw:	16	1	trace	3
6⅛" center slices	5	trace	trace	1
pickle, sweet, 1 med.	146	.5	trace	36.5
pickle, sour or dill:				
1 large	11	.5	trace	22
Eggplant, cooked: 1 cup	34	2	trace	7
Endive, raw: 1 cup	10	1	trace	2
(escarole, chicory)				
Belgian Endive, 4": 1	5	trace	trace	1
Kale, cooked: 1 cup	45	4	1	8
Kohlrabi, cooked: 1 cup	36	2.5	trace	8
Leeks, raw: 1 cup	104	4	.5	22
Lentils, cooked: 1 cup	212	15.5	trace	39.5
Lettuce, headed, raw:				
loose leaf, 4" diam.:				
1 head	30	3	trace	6
compact, 4¾" diam.:				
1 head	70	4	.5	12.5
2 large or 4 small leaves	5	1	trace	trace
Mushrooms, cooked or				
canned: 1 cup	41	4.5	trace	5.5
Okra, cooked: 8 pods	30	2	trace	6
Olives, green: 1 large	9	trace	1	trace
ripe: 1 large	13	trace	1.5	trace
Onions, mature:				
Raw, 2½" diam.:				
1 onion	50	2	trace	11
Cooked: 1 cup	80	2	trace	18
Onions, young green, small,				
no tops: 6 onions	25	trace	trace	5
Parsley, raw, chopped:				
1 tbs.	1	trace	trace	trace
Parsnips, cooked: 1 cup	95	2	1	22

FOODS: PORTION	CALORIES	PROTEIN (grams)	FAT (grams)	CARBO-HYDRATES (grams)
VEGETABLES (continued)				
Peas, green:				
cooked: 1 cup	110	8	1	19
canned, with liquid:				
1 cup	170	8	1	32
Peppers, sweet, green:				
1 medium	15	1	trace	3
sweet, red: 1 pod	20	1	trace	3
Potatoes, med. (about 3 lbs.):				
Baked, after peeling:				
1 potato	90	3	trace	21
Boiled, peeled after boiling:				
1 potato	105	3	trace	23
Boiled, peeled before boiling: 1 potato	90	3	trace	21
French fried, 1 piece 2″ x ½″ x ½″: 10 pieces	155	2	7	20
Mashed (with milk added): 1 cup	145	4	1	30
Chips, medium, 2″ diam.: 10 chips	110	1	7	10
Pumpkin, canned: 1 cup	83	2	1	18
Radishes, small: 4	10	trace	trace	2
Sauerkraut, canned, drained: 1 cup	30	2	trace	6
Soybeans, mature, cooked: 1 cup	277	22	11.5	21.5
immature, raw	284	22	10	26
Spinach, cooked: 1 cup	45	6	1	6
Squash, cooked:				
Summer, diced: 1 cup	35	1	trace	8
Winter, baked, mashed: 1 cup	126	3	.5	30
Summer, raw: 1 cup	38	2	trace	8
Sweet Potatoes:				
Baked (1 sweet potato 5″ x 2″)	155	2	1	36
Boiled (1 sweet potato 5″ x 2″)	170	2	1	39
Candied (1 sweet potato 3½″ x 2¼″)	295	2	6	60
Tomatoes:				
Raw, 1 medium 2″ x 2½″	30	2	trace	6
Canned, or cooked: 1 cup	45	2	trace	9
Tomato juice, canned: 1 cup	50	2	trace	9
Tomato catsup: 1 tbs.	15	trace	trace	4

FOODS: PORTION	CALORIES	PROTEIN (grams)	FAT (grams)	CARBO-HYDRATES (grams)
VEGETABLES (continued)				
Turnips, cooked, diced:				
1 cup	40	1	trace	9
Vegetable juice, cocktail, canned or bottled:				
6 oz.	31	1.5	trace	6.5
Water chestnuts, Chinese,				
raw: 4 average	20	trace	trace	4.5
Watercress: 1 cup	10	1	trace	1.5

CHEESE, CREAM, MILK, EGGS, AND RELATED PRODUCTS

FOODS: PORTION	CALORIES	PROTEIN (grams)	FAT (grams)	CARBO-HYDRATES (grams)
Cheese (1 ounce except where otherwise noted)				
American	106	6	9	.5
American Pimiento	106	6	9	.5
Blue	100	6	8	.5
Brie	95	6	8	trace
Camembert	85	6	7	trace
Cheddar	114	7	9.5	.5
Cottage, creamed:				
½ cup	117	14	5	3.5
uncreamed: ½ cup	96	19.5	.5	2
pot cheese, low-fat 2% fat: ½ cup	101	15.5	2	4
pot cheese, low-fat, 1% fat: ½ cup	82	14	1	3
Cream	99	2	10	1
Edam	101	7	8	.5
Feta	75	4	6	1
Fontina	110	7	9	.5
Gouda	101	7	8	.5
Limburger	93	6	8	trace
Monterey	106	7.0	8.5	trace
Mozzarella	80	5.5	6	.5
Mozzarella, part skim	72	7	4.5	1
Muenster	104	6.5	8.5	.5
Neufchâtel	74	3	6.5	1
Parmesan grated	111	10	7.5	1
1 tbs.	23	2	1.5	trace
Port du Salut	100	6.5	8	trace
Ricotta: ½ cup	216	14	16	4
Ricotta, part skim: ½ cup	171	14	10	6.5
Romano	110	9	7.5	1.0
Roquefort	105	6	8.5	.5
Swiss:				
Natural, domestic	107	8	7.5	4.0
Processed	95	7	7	.5
Cheese Food, American	94	5.5	7	2.5

FOODS: PORTION	CALORIES	PROTEIN (grams)	FAT (grams)	CARBO-HYDRATES (grams)
CHEESE, CREAM, MILK, EGGS, AND RELATED PRODUCTS				
Cheese (continued)				
Cheese Spread, American	82	4.5	6.0	2.5
Cream:				
Cream, 1 tbs.				
half and half	20	.5	1.5	.5
light, table or coffee	29	.5	3	.5
medium (25% fat)	37	.5	4	.5
sour	26	.5	2.5	.5
sour, imitation, cultured	20	.5	2	.5
whipping cream topping	8	trace	1	.5
whipping, heavy, whipped	26	trace	3	trace
whipping, heavy, unwhipped	52	.5	5.5	.5
whipping, light, whipped	22	trace	2.5	trace
whipping, light, unwhipped	44	.5	4.5	.5
Creamer:				
liquid, frozen: ½ oz.	20	trace	2.0	1.5
Nondairy, powder: 1 tsp.	11	trace	1	1
Milk, canned, undiluted: 1 fl. oz.				
Condensed, sweetened	123	3.0	3.5	21
evaporated, whole, unsweetened: 1 fl. oz.	42	2	2.5	3
evaporated, skim, canned: 1 fl. oz.	25	2.5	trace	3.5
milk, dry, skim:				
nonfat solids: ¼ cup	109	11	trace	15.5
whole	159	8.5	8.5	12.5
Fresh (1 cup): 8 fl. oz.:				
Buttermilk, cultured, skim	99	8	2	12
Skim	86	8.5	.5	12
Skimmed partially 1% fat	102	8.0	2.5	11.5
Skimmed partially 2% fat	125	8.5	4.5	12
Whole, 3.7% fat	157	8.0	.9	11.5
Yogurt, plain, low-fat: 1 cup	120	8.0	4.0	13
whole milk: 1 cup	139	8	7.5	10.5
Eggs, chicken, raw or cooked without fat:				
white only from 1 large egg	16	3.5	trace	.5
whole, 1 large	79	6	5.5	.5

FOODS: PORTION	CALORIES	PROTEIN (grams)	FAT (grams)	CARBO-HYDRATES (grams)
CHEESE, CREAM, MILK, EGGS, AND RELATED PRODUCTS				
Eggs (continued)				
yolk only from 1 large egg	63	3	5.5	trace
Eggs, dried, whole: 2 tbs.	60	4.5	4	.5
GRAIN PRODUCTS: BREADS, CEREALS, GRAINS, CAKES				
Barley, pearled, uncooked: 1 cup	782	18	2	173
Biscuits baking powder 2½″ diam.: 1 biscuit	138	3	6.5	17
Bran flakes (40% bran): 1 oz.	87	3	.5	18
Breads:				
Cracked wheat (20 slices per lb.): 1 slice	60	2	1	12
French, enriched: 1 slice	58	2	.5	11
Italian, enriched: 1 slice	55	2	trace	11
Protein: 1 slice	45	2.5	0	8.5
Pumpernickel, dark: 1 slice	56	2	trace	12
Raisin (20 per loaf): 1 slice	60	2	1	12
Rye, light: 1 slice	55	2	trace	12
White, enriched (20 per lb.): 1 slice	60	2	1	12
(26 per lb.): 1 slice	45	1	1	9
Whole wheat, graham all-wheat bread (20 per lb.): 1 slice	55	2	1	11
Breadcrumbs, dry, grated: 1 cup	345	11	4	65
Cakes:				
Angel food cake: 2″ section of 8″ cake	110	3	trace	23
Chocolate, fudge 2″ section of 10″ cake	420	5	14	70
Fruitcake, dark 2″ x 2″ x ½″: 1 piece	105	2	4	17
Gingerbread, 2″ x 2″ x 2″: 1 piece	180	2	7	28
Cupcake, plain, 2¾″ diam.: 1 cake	160	3	3	31
Poundcake, 2¾″ x 3″ x ⅝″: Slice	130	2	7	16
Sponge, 2″ sector, 8″ diam. cake: 1 section	115	3	2	22

FOODS: PORTION	CALORIES	PROTEIN (grams)	FAT (grams)	CARBO-HYDRATES (grams)
GRAIN PRODUCTS: BREADS, CEREALS, GRAINS, CAKES				
Cookies:				
Plain and assorted 3" diam. 1 cookie	110	2	3	19
Fig bars, small: 1	55	1	1	12
Corn flakes, enriched:				
1 cup	93	2	trace	21
Plain: 1 oz.	110	2	trace	24
Presweetened: 1 oz.	115	1	trace	26
Cornmeal, white or yellow, dry: 1 cup	420	11	5	87
Corn Muffins, 2¾" diameter: 1	155	4	5	22
Corn, puffed, presweetened, enriched: 1 oz.	100	1	trace	26
Crackers:				
Graham 4 small or 2 medium	55	1	1	10
Saltines, 2" square: 2 crackers	35	1	1	6
Soda, plain, 2½" square: 2 crackers	45	1	1	8
Crackermeal: 1 tbs.	45	1	1	7
Doughnuts, cake type: 1	135	2	7	17
Farina, enriched, cooked: 1 cup	105	3	trace	22
Macaroni, cooked until tender: 1 cup	155	5	1	32
Melba toast: 1 slice	15	.5	trace	2.5
Muffin, with enriched white flour: 2¾" diam.	135	4	5	19
Noodles (egg) cooked, enriched: 1 cup	200	7	2	37
Oatmeal or rolled oats, cooked: 1 cup	150	5	3	26
Pancakes, 4" diam.:				
1 cake	60	2	2	8
Buckwheat: 1 cake	45	2	2	6
Piecrust, enriched, 9" crust: 1 crust	655	10	36	72
Pie, 4" sector of 9" diam.:				
Apple; Cherry: 1 Sector	330	3	13	53
Custard: 1 Sector	265	7	11	34
Lemon meringue: 1 Sector	300	4	12	45
Mince: 1 Sector	340	3	9	62
Pumpkin: 1 Sector	265	5	12	34
Pizza (Cheese), 5½" sector, ⅛ of 14" pie: 1 Sector	180	8	6	23

FOODS: PORTION	CALORIES	PROTEIN (grams)	FAT (grams)	CARBO-HYDRATES (grams)
GRAIN PRODUCTS: BREADS, CEREALS, GRAINS, CAKES				
Popcorn, popped: 1 cup	55	2	1	11
Rice, cooked:				
Parboiled: 1 cup	205	4	trace	45
White: 1 cup	200	4	trace	44
Rice, puffed, enriched:				
1 cup	55	1	trace	12
Rice flakes, enriched:				
1 cup	115	2	trace	26
Rolls, 12 per pound:				
1 roll	115	3	2	20
Hard, round, 2 oz.				
ea.: 1 roll	160	5	2	31
Rye Wafers, 1⅞" x 3½":				
2 wafers	45	2	trace	10
Spaghetti, cooked until				
tender: 1 cup	155	5	1	32
Wheat, puffed, enriched:				
1 oz.	100	4	trace	22
presweetened: 1 oz.	105	1	trace	26
Wheat, shredded, plain:				
1 oz.	100	4	.5	21
Wheat flakes: 1 oz.	100	3	trace	23
Wheat flours:				
Whole wheat: 1 cup	420	16	2	85
All purpose sifted: 1 cup	400	12	1	84
Self-rising: 1 cup	385	10	1	81
Wheat germ: 1 tbs.	24	12	.5	2.5
SUGARS, SWEETS, NUTS				
Almonds, shelled: 1 cup	900	26	77	28
Brazil nuts, broken				
pieces: 1 cup	970	20	92	15
Candy:				
Caramels: 1 oz.	120	1	3	22
Chocolate, sweetened,				
milk: 1 oz.	145	2	9	16
Fudge, plain: 1 oz.	115	trace	3	23
Hard candy: 1 oz.	110	0	0	28
Marshmallow: 1 oz.	95	1	0	23
Cashew nuts, roasted:				
1 cup	570	15	45	26
Coconut, dried, shredded,				
sweetened: 1 oz.	156	1	11	15
Gelatin, dry, plain: 1 tbs.	35	9	trace	0
Gelatin dessert, prepared:				
Plain: 1 cup	155	4	trace	36
With fruit: 1 cup	180	3	trace	42

FOODS: PORTION	CALORIES	PROTEIN (grams)	FAT (grams)	CARBO-HYDRATES (grams)
SUGARS, SWEETS, NUTS				
Peanuts, roasted, shelled:				
Halves: 1 cup	885	37	69	29
Chopped: 1 tbs.	52	2	4	2
Peanut Butter: 1 tbs.	93	4	8	3
Pecans:				
Halves: 1 cup	760	10	74	15
Chopped: 1 tbs.	50	1	5	1
Sherbet: 1 cup	235	3	trace	58
Sugar: 1 oz.	110	0	0	28
Walnuts, chopped: 1 cup	790	17	73	18
1 tbs.	50	1	4.5	1
BEVERAGES				
Alcoholic:				
Beer, canned or bottled:				
Regular: 12 fl. oz.	150	1	0	12.5
Low Calorie:				
12 fl. oz. under	100	1	0	3
Distilled liquor:				
Unflavored bourbon, brandy, Canadian whiskey, gin, Irish whiskey, Scotch whiskey, rum, rye whiskey, tequila, vodka 1 fl. oz.	65–82*	0	0	trace
Wines:				
Dessert (18.8% alcohol): 3 oz.	117	trace	0	6.5
Dry (12.2% alcohol): 3 oz.	75	trace	0	3.5
Carbonated (nonalcoholic):				
Sweetened (quinine sodas): 8 oz.	71	0	0	18
Unsweetened (club soda)	0	0	0	0
Cola type: 8 oz.	89	0	0	23
Flavored sodas:				
sweetened: 8 oz.	105	0	0	27
unsweetened (diet sodas): 8 oz.	—	—	—	—
Ginger ale, pale dry and golden: 8 oz.	71	—	—	18
Root beer: 8 oz.	94	—	—	24
Coffee: 1 cup	2	trace	trace	.5
Tea: 1 cup	2	trace	trace	.5

*Calories average 70 for 86 proof; may vary up or down as indicated if higher or lower proof.

FOODS: PORTION	CALORIES	PROTEIN (grams)	FAT (grams)	CARBO-HYDRATES (grams)
FATS, OILS, AND SHORTENINGS				
Butter, 4 sticks per lb.				
2 sticks = 1 cup.	1,626	2	184	trace
⅛ stick = 1 tbs.	100	trace	11	trace
1 pat (90 per lb.)	36	trace	4	trace
Fats, cooking:				
Bacon fat, chicken fat:				
1 tbs.	126	0	14	0
Lard: 1 cup	1,985	1	220	0
1 tbs.	124	0	14	0
Margarine, 4 sticks per lb.				
2 sticks = 1 cup	1,633	1.5	183	1
⅛ stick = 1 tbs.	102	trace	11	trace
1 pat (80 per lb.)	36	trace	4	trace
Oils, salad or cooking: corn, cottonseed, olive, soybean, peanut, safflower oils: 1 tbs.	125	0	14	0
Salad dressings:				
Blue cheese: 1 tbs.	90	1	10	.5
Imitation mayonnaise type: 1 tbs.	60	trace	6	2
French: 1 tbs.	60	trace	6	2
Mayonnaise: 1 tbs.	110	trace	12	trace
Thousand Island: 1 tbs.	75	trace	8	1
MISCELLANEOUS ITEMS				
Bouillon cube, ⅝": 1	5	2	trace	trace
Catsup, tomato: 1 tbs.	19	trace	trace	4.5
Chili sauce (mostly tomatoes): 1 tbs.	15	trace	trace	4
Chocolate:				
Bitter or unsweetened: 1 oz.	144	3	17.5	8
Sweetened: 1 oz.	151	1	10	16.5
Chocolate Syrup: 1 tbs.	40	trace	trace	11
Hollandaise sauce: 1 tbs.	48	1	4	2
Honey, strained or extracted: 1 tbs.	64	trace	0	17
Jams, marmalades, preserves: 1 tbs.	55	trace	trace	14
Jellies: 1 tbs.	50	0	0	13
Soups, canned, ready to serve:				
Bean: 1 cup	190	8	5	30
Beef: 1 cup	100	6	4	11

FOODS: PORTION	CALORIES	PROTEIN (grams)	FAT (grams)	CARBO-HYDRATES (grams)
MISCELLANEOUS ITEMS				
Soups (continued)				
Bouillon, broth, consomme: 1 cup	10	2	—	0
Clam chowder: 1 cup	85	5	2	12
Cream soup (asparagus, celery, mushroom): 1 cup	200	7	12	18
Noodle, rice, barley: 1 cup	115	6	4	13
Pea: 1 cup	140	6	2	25
Tomato (with water): 1 cup	86	2	2	15
Vegetable: 1 cup	80	5	2	10
Syrup, table blends: 1 tbs.	55	0	0	15
Sugar, granulated, cane, or beet: 1 cup	770	0	0	199
1 tbs.	48	0	0	12
Lump, 1⅛″ x ⅝″ x ⅛″: 1 lump	25	0	0	7
Powdered (stirred up): 1 cup	495	0	0	127
Brown, firm-packed: 1 cup	820	0	0	210
1 tbs.	51	0	0	13
Vinegar: 1 tbs.	2	0	0	1
White Sauce, medium: 1 cup	430	10	33	23

15
Shape Up and Count Your Blessings

We are fortunate to be living in what I feel is a golden age—in the greatest country in the world. Opportunities are unlimited. Food is plentiful. Vital statistics predict a long life. We must be intelligent enough to enjoy and make the most of all our blessings. A big part of that for you is to keep in shape—trim, active, and in excellent health.

The changes that have taken place in medicine since I graduated from medical school in 1933 have been miraculous. They compare very favorably with the modern miracles of radio, color television, lasers, atomic power, space travel, and air travel, which the young take so much for granted.

In my medical school days, there was a thin book called *Useful Drugs,* which contained about twenty medications that had specific and useful therapeutic effects. There are now literally hundreds. As examples, except for insulin, thyroid, and adrenalin, we had few of the miraculous hormones now available.

Antibiotics came in with sulfa in 1936, and penicillin about 1941. There are now enough different antibiotics to choose from to justify the subspecialty of "infectious diseases." Vaccines of various kinds have eliminated the horror of polio and a host of other viral and bacterial illnesses.

Advances in diagnosis (CAT scan, isotopes, laminography, arterial-catherization, arteriography, etc.), anesthesia, anticoagulants, and antibiotics, have made complicated surgical procedures routine. These include lung resections, intricate brain procedures, renal dialysis, joint replacements, heart valve replacements, coronary artery bypass for angina, many more.

Diuretics and our knowledge of the importance of

sodium have made the treatment of congestive failure most effective—so that we can now delete the word "dropsy" from the medical lexicon. The cardiac care units, electric shock, cardioversion machines, and pacemakers, are marvels no one could have contemplated thirty years ago.

These innumerable drugs and surgical procedures now make it possible to cure and give comfort to over 95 percent of patients seen in the office.

It is not so long ago that Osler, one of the great internists of all time, encouraged the physician to be patient, understanding, and tender, since that was about all he could offer therapeutically. The great challenge of the time was bedside diagnosis.

It is not generally realized how important the pharmaceutical companies have been in the progress that medicine has made. They are often accused of making inordinate profits, with very little concern for the public. While the costs involved in the cure of an acute illness may seem exorbitant, they cannot be compared with the time and hospital expense they have *avoided*. It is the chronic illness that unfortunately becomes a burden, in spite of the relief afforded.

The government and the public have both been remiss, I believe, in not recognizing and expressing gratitude for the great advances that this industry has made in the western world in the past forty years.

The exciting privilege of witnessing the phenomenal medical and surgical advances over these years has made it possible for me to approach many problems in a simple, fundamental manner.

I hope the discussion of medical problems, and the various diets presented in this book, will provide comfort and help to many of you. I wish you good health, good living and a long, happy life.

Herman Tarnower

M.D., FACP, D-IM (cv)

The Medical Appendix

You and Your Physician—Some Medical Problems That Are Affected by Diet

CONGESTIVE HEART FAILURE . . . FOOD ALLERGIES . . . DIABETES . . . ARTERIOSCLEROSIS . . . DIVERTICULOSIS AND DIVERTICULITIS . . . HYPERTENSION (HIGH BLOOD PRESSURE) . . . PEPTIC ULCER . . . PYROSIS (INDIGESTION, HEARTBURN) . . . GALL BLADDER . . . CONSTIPATION

To the reader: This chapter is addressed primarily to the physician, but if you wish to read "over the doctor's shoulder," this material may be of interest to you. I must emphasize that all diseases, any deviation from normal, any problem outside the range of normal health, including weight problems, *must be treated and supervised by your physician*—avoid self-treatment or self-medication.

TO THE PHYSICIAN

Forty-five years of practice have been busy, fulfilling, and exciting. The great advances in medicine and surgery now make it possible to cure or comfort over 95 percent of patients seen in the office.

One of the discouraging aspects of the great progress made is that simple problems are too often complicated unnecessarily. Reliance on clinical judgment in a rather easy situation frequently is snarled by multiple laboratory procedures—an attempt to confirm the obvious (also very expensive and time-consuming).

The well-trained physician finds it difficult to discard the academic, ivory tower approach in the practical care of a patient. This approach is also apt to manifest itself when diet is an important element in the diagnosis and treatment of disease. I believe in the empirical approach. Over the years, through trial and error, I have accumulated a number of diets and procedures that patients with special problems have found easy and helpful to follow under my supervision.

This book does not pretend to be an academic or scientific documentation of the diagnosis and treatment of disease. It describes the practical approach to a few common medical problems, in an effort to educate the public and stimulate the medical profession to adopt simple medical procedures, wherever possible.

Congestive Heart Failure

As a result of various kinds of "strain," the heart muscle is sometimes unable to maintain a satisfactory circulation. This can cause swelling of the feet, the accumulation of fluid in the lungs (shortness of breath), or other parts of the body (swelling of the liver, etc.). This is called congestive heart failure, and is treated much the same way no matter what type of heart disease has caused it.

It is imperative that every heart patient be educated on how to avoid *acute heart failure;* that is, the severe sudden onset of shortness of breath. This can be accomplished irrespective of the type of heart disease, whether it be congenital, valvular, hypertensive, or myocardial infarction (coronary disease). I give each of my heart patients an outline describing in lay terms the nature of his illness, what symptoms he may expect, and how he can and must cooperate in the management of his illness.

These are the points I emphasize:

1. DAILY WEIGHT CONTROL

The most valuable instrument in the diagnosis, care, and treatment of congestive heart failure is a *good scale*. The patient must weigh daily, before breakfast, and keep an accurate weight diary. In the cardiac, a gain in weight usually indicates an excess accumulation of fluid. Each pint of water weighs approximately one pound. A two-pound increase in weight could thus indicate the accumulation of approximately a quart of fluid. Since there is no certain way of knowing whether the added weight is flesh or fluid, the patient should be instructed on how to take a diuretic to help determine this. Where rapid resolution is indicated a diuretic may be given by injection. If weight increase has been due to fluid, it will be passed as urine.

2. SALT IN THE DIET

When circulation is impaired, the kidneys are unable to excrete salt and fluids properly. It is impossible by any investigation, simple or complicated, to determine exactly how much salt (sodium) a particular heart patient can safely handle. We only know that the sodium ion holds water in body fluids and tissues.

No patient who may develop acute heart failure should add salt at the table. Trial and error through weight variations and careful observation will determine whether, and to what extent, the salt in the cooking should be restricted. For the individual with Class III and IV heart disease (very serious), the cooking may have to be as salt-free as possible. (See list of "Permitted" and "Prohibited" Foods.) Salt substitutes without sodium may be used.

Before we understood the importance of salt (sodium) and before effective diuretics, the only way we had of eliminating excess body fluid to give relief from shortness of breath, was to tap the fluid as it accumulated in the chest. As an intern at Bellevue Hospital in New York City back in 1933. my daily rounds always required the tapping of four to eight chests.

I had the privilege of being present when the first scientific paper on the importance of sodium was delivered, at the Association of American Physicians in Atlantic City in 1939, by Dr. H. A. Schroeder of the Rockefeller Institute. It was an exciting, revolutionary concept. Prior to that address, we restricted the fluid intake of heart patients to 800 cc a day, regardless of the misery this caused. Today there is no need for any heart patient, no matter how ill, to be edematous (accumulate excess fluid), or to be short of breath.

3. DIURETICS

The proper use of modern diuretics has made it very rare for a patient, even with severe heart damage, to have his food so salt-free that it is virtually tasteless and inedible. The list of acceptable herbs provided here can also be useful in making food more palatable.

A number of safe oral diuretics can be administered daily or several times a week to help the kidney excrete salt and water. These drugs often make it possible for heart patients to have a nearly normal amount of salt in their food. The diuretic dosage will vary with the cardiac efficiency and the amount of salt ingested.

The patient's weight curve, followed daily, will be a guide for diuretic intake. A diuretic is taken as soon as weight rises by as much as two pounds. *Don't wait for shortness of breath or swollen ankles.* The maintenance diuretic dosage is finally easily determined by this procedure.

4. DIGITALIS

This drug increases the efficiency of the heart muscle. It must never be stopped or increased without the physician's consent.

5. POTASSIUM CHLORIDE

A low level of potassium in the body causes muscular weakness, and occasionally, nausea. Potassium loss is apt to occur when diuretics are given over a long period of time. When this occurs, potassium chloride is administered by mouth—rarely by injection. (See list of foods high in potassium, at the end of this section.)

When congestive heart failure has responded to these measures, the heart muscle can then maintain a satisfactory circulation, and the patient may be able to resume most of his usual activities. In fact, with proper

THE MEDICAL APPENDIX 185

managment, cardiac efficiency will very often improve.

With our present knowledge, and the therapeutic agents available, it is possible to keep patients comfortable, with very rare exceptions, no matter how severe the heart disease.

6. REST AND ACTIVITY

Patients with congestive heart failure need rest; that is, restriction in activity. This does not mean they have to go to bed. In fact, most patients are more comfortable sitting up in a chair and, in the majority of instances, all that is required is some moderate restriction in activity.

The question most commonly asked by the patient is *"How much and what can I do?" As your doctor will tell you, the answer is simple and easy to understand. Anything you can do comfortably, that means without shortness of breath, pain, or undue fatigue, you can do safely; the more you do the better. Avoid competitive sports, or any situation over which you don't have complete control. No stress test is as simple, or as valuable, as a patient's intelligent use of this advice.*

FOODS PERMITTED ON SODIUM-RESTRICTED DIETS

Fresh vegetables, cooked or raw.

All fresh meats, poultry, or game. Also fish, though fresh fish should be soaked for ½ hour in ice water before cooking, because it is often shipped packed in salt.

All fruits, raw or cooked, including canned fruits, jellies, and jams.

Hardtack and Jewish unleavened bread (matzos).

Home-baked pies and cakes. Use only calcium phosphate baking powder.

Raw clams and oysters; crab, lobster, shrimp, scallops.

Ginger ale.

Milk limited to one glass a day.

For flavorings, see list that follows.

Sample restaurant menu: First course raw oysters or clams with lemon juice; fruit cup or melon (without prosciutto). The entree should be fish, fowl or meat that can be cooked to order without salt, a baked potato, and one vegetable which probably will have some salt. Dessert—sherbet, fresh or stewed fruit. Use sweet butter only, if any.

FOODS PROHIBITED WHERE SEVERE SODIUM RESTRICTION IS INDICATED

Use minimum amount of salt in cooking; do not add salt at table.

No seasonings containing sodium, such as onion, garlic, and celery salt; no monosodium glutamate (MSG).

No salt butter or margarine.

No salted, dried, smoked, tinned, or pickled meats or fish, no corned beef, ham, bacon, salt pork, smoked salmon, sausage, bologna, salami, pastrami, tongue, frankfurters.

No canned vegetables unless labeled "salt-free pack."

No commercial soups, either in cans or dry; no bouillon cubes or packets.

No canned or frozen meals, including TV dinners, or prepared spaghetti and sauces.

No hors d'oeuvres or canapes.

No cheese, except plain salt-free cream cheese, or salt-free cottage cheese.

No olives, green or ripe.

No pickles, relish, sauerkraut.

No salted nuts, salted crackers, pretzels, potato chips, salted popcorn, salted snacks. In fact, all crackers and cookies should be banned, as many have baking soda in them.

No peanut butter (unless low sodium dietetic).

No dry (ready to eat) cereals allowed except shredded wheat.

No ordinary bread or rolls.

No packaged, commercially prepared cocktail sauce, ketchup, mustard, mayonnaise, salad dressing, soy sauce, commercial butter sauce, Worcestershire, horseradish, and other piquant sauces; no meat tenderizers, extracts, or sauces; no commercial syrups or molasses.

No soda bicarb, soda mints, baking soda, and no proprietary medicines that have salt as one of the ingredients (check labels).

Many effervescent drinks contain sodium and are forbidden, especially club soda—unless it is labeled "salt-free."

No packaged, commercially prepared mixes for rolls, biscuits, pancakes, or cakes.

SEASONINGS, SPICES, HERBS PERMITTED ON SODIUM-RESTRICTED DIETS

Allspice
Almond extract
Anise
Basil
Bay leaf
Bouillon cube, *low-sodium* dietetic if less than 5 mg sodium per cube
Caraway
Cardamom
Catsup, *dietetic only*
Cayenne
Chervil
Chili powder
Chives
Cinnamon
Cloves
Cocoa (1 to 2 teaspoons)
Coconut
Coriander seeds
Cumin
Curry powder
Dill
Fennel
Garlic
Ginger
Honey
Horseradish root or horseradish *prepared without salt*
Juniper
Ketchup, *dietetic only*
Lemon juice
Lime juice
Mace
Maple extract
Marjoram
Meat extract, *low-sodium dietetic only*
Meat tenderizers, *low-sodium dietetic only*
Mint
Mustard, *dry only*
Nutmeg
Onion, fresh, in any form
Orange extract
Oregano
Paprika
Parsley
Pepper, fresh—green or red
Pepper, black, red, white
Peppermint extract
Pimiento

Poppy seed
Purslane
Rosemary
Saffron
Sage
Savory
Sesame seeds
Sorrel

Sugar substitutes
Tarragon
Thyme
Turmeric
Vanilla extract
Vinegar
Wine, as flavoring
Walnut extract

FOODS HIGH IN POTASSIUM

Apricots
Asparagus
Banana
Beef
Broccoli
Brussels sprouts
Cantaloupe
Chicken
Fish
Figs
Grapefruit
Grapefruit juice
Lamb

Milk, skim and whole
Nuts, unsalted
Potato
Prune juice
Prunes, uncooked
Orange
Orange juice
Raisins
Tomato
Tuna, canned
Turkey
Yams

I cannot emphasize too strongly, and this your doctor will confirm, that only trial and error can determine just how strict the salt restriction must be.

Food Allergies

Allergies are fascinating to treat. Some are easily identified and treated; some require the most sophisticated medical sleuthing. In observing or experiencing allergies, even the layman can get some idea of how complicated and unpredictable our body chemistry can be.

A high index of suspicion is the most important ingredient for diagnosing allergies. An itchy eye could mean you've been rubbing it and something on your hand now makes it itch, perhaps nail polish. A chronic skin rash on the hands could mean sensitivity to a detergent.

But these are easy. The possibilities are almost infinite. Specialists, because of their wide experience, can often find the guilty ingredient in places one wouldn't think to look.

Chronic headaches, recurrent abdominal pain, episodic diarrhea and occasionally chronic diarrhea, urticaria (hives), and a host of other maladies, are often symptoms of food allergy. Skin tests to find the source of the allergy are often disappointing.

The Allergy Elimination Diet that follows is simple, and very useful. Its concept was originated twenty years ago by Dr. Walter C. Alvarez, a distinguished Mayo Clinic internist. His diagnostic and therapeutic approach to all diseases was simple, exciting, and very often effective where many other physicians of great renown were unsuccessful.

When one suspects that a food allergy is the cause of a patient's symptoms, the Allergy Elimination Diet should be meticulously adhered to for three days. Lack of relief by the end of three days will, in most instances, rule out *food* as the cause of the symptoms. If the headache, hives, and other symptoms subside during the three days, the patient then should gradually add different foods each day in an attempt to identify the offending agent. I am assuming you are under a doctor's supervision, of course.

An allergic response to a food one eats only infrequently is easy to identify—like hives due to lobster. Symptoms due to food sensitivity will occur within three to four hours after ingestion. Allergy to more widely used foods are not as easy to trace. A person who is allergic to chicken, for example, may become ill from a vegetable soup, unaware that chicken stock was used in preparing it. Someone sensitive to milk can go into shock simply by eating a little Roquefort cheese in salad dressing.

Successful completion of good dieting detective work can be most gratifying for the internist, and an indescribable relief to the patient. Not infrequently, allergy patients have been considered psychoneurotic, or their headache problem is labeled "migraine." Such misdiagnoses are often cover-ups for an inability to find a medical reason for the patient's complaints.

I think of a case where a patient had her appendix removed. It was a simple operation but her recovery was slow. She had recurring episodes of vomiting and abdominal pain. Eggnogs had been prescribed to "build her up." When it was finally recognized that her symptoms recurred each day, a half-hour after her eggnog, her problem was solved. Significantly, she had been slated for psychiatric help, with the thought that her problem might be emotional, since no clinical basis for her physical complaints could be found.

ALLERGY ELIMINATION DIET

The following Allergy Elimination Diet is a simple way of ruling out food allergy. The diet is to be followed *exactly* for three full days.

Breakfast Each Day

Oatmeal with a little butter or sugar.

Lunch and Supper Each Day

Lamb chop or loin of lamb, either broiled or roasted or fried with butter.
Carrots and rice with butter.

Beverages Allowed

Only water; no milk, coffee, tea, sodas.

Dessert

Stewed pears or peaches.
Do not use laxatives or chewing gum.

Remember that the point of this diet is not to help the patient lose weight, but to discover what is making her sick. If she still has the allergy symptoms at the end of the three-day diet, you can pretty well rule out food as their cause.

If the symptoms have subsided during the three days, then begin adding new foods very gradually. Milk, eggs, wheat, shellfish, and chocolate are among the most common causes of allergies, so it makes sense to test them early. To complicate things, sometimes more than one food can be causing the problems.

CASE HISTORIES ON THE ALLERGY ELIMINATION DIET

At this point I include some actual case histories of a few of my allergy patients to give a clearer picture of the wide variety of problems and solutions in allergy cases.

CASE A: "Immediately after the birth of my first child, I began to get headaches. These would occur at any time. Dr. T. suggested that the headaches might be related to what I ate. I went on his Allergy Elimination Diet for three days—and didn't have any headaches.

"I added a few new foods daily, and was still fine. When I added eggs, the headaches recurred. I did this three times, to be certain.

"I eliminated eggs from my diet for six months. Then Dr. T suggested that I try very small amounts of egg. After a while, I was able to tolerate them again.

"Five years later, I gave birth to my second child, and I developed the same allergy to eggs. Once again I eliminated eggs and egg products from my diet. This worked. Later I was able to reintroduce eggs the same way."

CASE B: "Almost 20 years ago, I had frequent attacks of vomiting and diarrhea. A doctor put me on a bland diet—eggnog and other items. No help. I became dehydrated. Went to a hospital, and was put on fluids. Then bland diet—eggs and milk. More vomiting and diarrhea, with severe stomach cramps.

"Several times, the dietician made mistakes and fed me a sandwich (I remember turkey). They let me go home—very weak and thin . . .

"I went to my parents' home to recuperate. Bland diet—more of the same symptoms. After several days, the pain was so bad that I was taken to another hospital in an ambulance. I was X-rayed, and a diagnosis of intestinal obstruction was made.

"I was operated on to relieve the obstruction. Put on a bland diet—again, vomiting, diarrhea, and abdominal cramps. Dr. T came to see me, questioned me carefully, and realized that my symptoms were directly related to the eggnogs I was taking. They were immediately forbidden.

"Since then I have avoided milk and eggs. Sometimes if I have a build-up (eat foods I know I shouldn't, such as pancakes, or pound cake), the symptoms recur. I tried milk one day, an ounce, but my heart pounded so badly, I never tried again."

CASE C: "At various intervals through the years, I suffered from acute ulcerlike symptoms, severe headaches, cramps, nausea, diarrhea, and general malaise. Neither gall bladder, GI series, nor a neurological examination, revealed any significant finding.

"I was advised to place myself on a bland diet. This diet consisted of such dairy products as cheeses, custards, and milk. My frantic mother insisted on 'fortifying' me daily with an eggnog. My symptoms continued.

"Years later, my two daughters began to manifest the same symptoms. I cautiously limited their diet to bland dairy products. Episodes of headache and nausea intensified. Any parent can envision my despair. One day, I mentioned this distressing situation to Dr. T.

"He was suspicious of a food allergy. My daughters and I tried the Allergy Elimination Diet. Morning headache, nausea, and tummy discomforts stopped. Within twenty-four hours, we were all symptom free. With that simple detective work, milk and dairy products were discovered to be the source of the trouble.

"Dr. T suggested that after six months, it might be possible to reintroduce small quantities of dairy products. I am happy to report that we are all enjoying good health. Whenever the old familiar symptoms begin to reappear, I quickly re-evaluate our diet."

CASE D: "My rash started in May 1976. It always started under my left arm or on my thighs. The rash first appeared as a series of small red blotches—shaped like the letter C, not raised. As the rash spread, it formed a circle or wreathlike shape. And as it moved from the center outward, the rash would spread in the same circular pattern while the center slowly cleared. New blotches were visible under the skin before they blossomed. Sometimes the rash was itchy.

"I consulted a dermatologist who treated me for about two months with no results. He prescribed antihistamines, cortisone ointment, and cortisone shots. The pills made me feel tired, dreary, and nervous. The shots were helpful in making the rash disappear, only to return a few days later if the shots were not repeated. A biopsy was taken to determine if the rash was an allergy fungisite. The tissue was sent to a laboratory where they found the tissue full of histamines.

"I was also examined by another dermatologist who gave me some kind of pills which made me quite ill (nervous, anxious, some shortness of breath). He tried a small dose but that didn't help me or the rash. Each doctor also did blood tests.

"In August, the rash was very severe and had spread under both arms, legs, thighs, and over both buttocks.

"My family doctor suggested that I take 8 mg of a cortisone medication orally every other day, plus antihistamines every day to get rid of the rash and not worry about the cause at this time. This cleared up the rash until the following February when the rash started again. A pediatric allergist friend thought that the rash might be a contact dermatitis. He suggested that I wear only cotton clothing and use only bland soap for laundry and personal use. This made no difference so I went back on the cortisone pills.

"In March I went to another dermatologist who

thought I had a reaction to a chemical. She suggested a special toothpaste and to avoid foods with artificial coloring or additives. She prescribed a medication which was slightly helpful. It seemed to stop the rash from spreading but did not clear it up. She then sent me to an allergist who also thought the rash was caused by a chemical. During this time I had all kinds of blood tests, lab tests, even a parasite stool test. All were negative. I was put back on cortisone—six 5 mg tablets a day. I was to cut the dosage every few days and continue to stay on the other medication. The rash finally disappeared in September.

"In April 1978 the rash returned. I started taking the tablets again, which helped. When the six 5 mg pills were cut down gradually to two 5 mg pills daily, the rash would return.

"In May, Dr. T became interested in my problem (being my husband's physician and now mine); he suggested that a definitive test should be made to determine once and for all whether the rash was food allergy related. He suggested a special limited diet for three days of: oatmeal, sugar, butter, rice, lamb, carrots and canned pears only (no coffee, no tea), and to continue the two 5 mg pills at the same time. After three days, the rash started to fade, and in another two days disappeared.

"Dr. T's instructions were to add one new food at a time in large quantities. If the new food did not cause the rash to return in 3–5 hours, it was safe. I added a new food every three or four days. I was able to discontinue the medication in a short time. After three months I discovered that any large amount of food with white flour, wheat flour or bran would cause the rash to appear. I also discovered that coffee distressed me.

"This, to the best of my recollection, is the history of 'My Rash.' I am convinced we are on the right track, and I am most grateful."

IN SUMMARY

The Allergy Elimination Diet is simple and inexpensive. You and your doctor will agree it is not only a valuable diagnostic and therapeutic procedure, but very often is the only realistic approach available.

Diverticulosis and Diverticulitis

Diverticulosis is probably the most common disorder of the large bowel. A colonic diverticulum is an abnormal outpouching or protrusion of the inner lining of the colon through the muscular coat of the colon. A single diverticulum may vary in size from a barely visible dimple to a sac two centimeters or more in diameter. Diverticulosis is the presence of two or more of these sacs; in many instances there are as many as a hundred.

NORMAL COLON

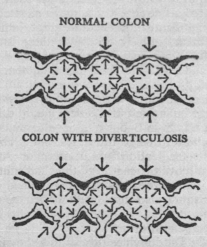

COLON WITH DIVERTICULOSIS

Diverticulitis is the infection of one or more of these sacs. It causes pain and tenderness over the area of inflammation, and may be accompanied by an elevated white blood count and fever. The condition requires emergency treatment. In the early stages the condition is easily treated medically. If neglected, it may go on to abscess formation and require extensive surgery.

I have seen dietary fads in diverticulitis go from no roughage to the popular, present-day concept of very high roughage diets. In my opinion, *diet is of little or no significance*. The experience of the sportsman, which follows, is not unusual. Too often, patients are given needless diet restrictions. If a patient feels that a particular food will cause an attack of diverticulitis, however, obviously it is prudent for him in such circumstances to avoid the offending food.

It is a useful rule of thumb for all to remember that any time an individual has abdominal pain accompanied by tenderness, he or she should seek medical treatment immediately. In fact, any abdominal tenderness should be considered a medical "emergency." Pain without tenderness, even severe, is rarely a serious emergency, but to be on the safe side, consult your physician.

The diagnosis of diverticulitis must be suspected, especially in the elderly, whenever there is lower abdominal pain with *tenderness* and, in rare instances, when the tenderness is in the upper abdomen.

My patients are told, under these circumstances, to avoid cathartics, and to start an antibiotic immediately. My choice, after years of successful use, in sulfadiazine, grams 1, t.i.d. In this book, I have carefully avoided recommendation of specific drugs, but my conviction here is so strong, I have made an exception.

The possibility of an allergy to sulfadiazine, as with any drug, must always be borne in mind. A rash is the most common allergic manifestation. Occasionally sulfadiazine may cause fever. Blood counts should be repeated every five days.

Obviously I am a maverick in this conviction. It is unfortunate, I think, that younger, well-trained, infectious disease specialists do not use sulfadiazine. They rely on the newer antibiotics which, in my opinion, are inferior in the treatment of this condition. Many of these doctors simply by virtue of age don't have the experience with the sulfa drugs that preceded our modern antibiotics.

Furthermore, it is extremely difficult to demonstrate the susceptibility of organisms to sulfa drugs because the media on which organisms are grown interferes with the sulfas' antibiotic action. My conviction about the use of sulfadiazine has grown out of long years of observing its successful results. I have never had a patient go to surgery for a ruptured diverticulum when the preceding advice was followed.

Occasionally patients have recurrent attacks of diverticulitis. In such instances, sulfadiazine .5 grams A.M. and P.M. will frequently be required to keep the diverticulitis under control. I have had patients on this routine for over twenty years, with good results.

TYPICAL CASE HISTORIES

A few words tell the story of a woman who suffered from diverticulitis, and followed the regimen described here. When they were vacationing, her husband sent me this postcard: "Ann was a good girl, followed your advice, recovered, and now rides horseback daily at this dude ranch." Ann added a postscript: "No fever. No tenderness. Feeling great. Many thanks."

A sportsman reports: "There is an old expression in life—'you get what you pay for'—but there are exceptions to this rule. Two years ago, I received some gratuitous advice from Dr. T which not only saved my life, but made it possible to enjoy it and to enjoy eating after eight years of strict diet, and about 16 months of hospitalization. In 1968, I had three operations which pretty well immobilized me for a year. Each one took three weeks in the hospital and three more weeks to recover.

"Starting in 1970, I had about three to four two-week bouts with diverticulitis, all painful and disrupting. Oral antibiotics did no good so I had to receive them intravenously. Dr. T simply said, 'Try sulfadiazine—it's the only thing we had to work with during the war, and no patient of mine ever perforated.' Mine had already perforated, causing peritonitis.

"Over Christmas and New Year's of 1976, I had three weeks in the hospital. In February of '76, while bone fishing in the Yucatan wilderness, I had another attack, but this time I was armed with 500 mg tablets of sulfadiazine. I took six tablets during the night, and six the next day.

"When I returned, I immediately had a white blood count of 6,500, while previously it would show 10,000 and 15,000. There is an expression, 'Doctors bury their mistakes, and architects (that's me) grow ivy.'

"Since my February and April attacks, cured with sulfa, I have been able to eat all roughage: celery, peas, lima beans, cabbage, and even nuts. My bowel movements, which for eight years were difficult, have been completely normal."

The experience I had with a close friend of mine, who is also my dentist, illustrates an interesting, fairly common, dilemma. Dr. H came to the office early one morning to tell me that he had been having right lower abdominal pain for five days. Examination disclosed tenderness and slight resistance in that area. The white count was 10,000 elevated from his usual count of about 6,000.

In a younger individual with these classic symptoms and signs of appendictis, an appendectomy would certainly have been indicated. I explained the situation to Dr. H and suggested that I treat him with sulfadiazine on the assumption that he might have diverticulitis involving the right colon. Even if it were appendicitis, there was a good chance that the drug would prevent surgery.

On the other hand, if surgery disclosed diverticulitis, he might become involved in a complicated surgical procedure that could lay him up for some time. A ruptured appendix was also a serious possibility, but

I felt sulfadiazine would contain such a situation to a reasonable risk.

In two days he was symptom-free. Three weeks later a barium enema demonstrated diverticulae of the ascending colon. That was in 1972 and there have been no recurrences.

Another case, as related by a patient: "One month after an attack of diverticulitis, X-rays showed the presence of diverticulosis. I was concerned, since I had several friends wtih similar ailments, all of whom suffered intensely at times. One died after several operations, and others were thoroughly inconvenienced with the malady and operations.

"Dr. T prescribed two sulfadiazine tablets three times a day for the acute attack, which lasted two days. Furthermore, I was advised—in the event of the recurrence of abdominal pain with tenderness—to take two sulfa tablets three times a day, and to contact Dr. T or any other physician, if traveling.

"At the advice of Dr. T, I always carry a prescription for sulfa on trips out of my home area. On several occasions when I had trouble, I used the sulfadiazine as directed. In the eighteen years, I have had no serious problems."

Diabetes Mellitus

Recent research postulates several very complicated causes or mechanisms for this disease. There is still a wide diversity of opinion as to a definition of diabetes mellitus. Essentially it is an inability to burn or use glucose properly so that the glucose rises in the bloodstream to abnormal levels and spills into the urine.

Insulin is the hormone necessary for proper glucose metabolism. In some diabetics there is an absolute insulin deficiency. In others, the deficiency varies.

For diabetics, diet is of primary importance. Very involved and difficult diets were once prescribed for them, and unfortunately these are still employed by some physicians and specialists. They require careful weighing of all foods and the elaborate percentage calculation of carbohydrate, fat, and protein. A sensible diabetic diet does not require these extreme measures except in the most unusual cases.

The large majority of adult diabetics are ketosis-free and overweight. Many of them may not even be aware that they are diabetic if symptoms are minimal, and variations in blood sugar are not dramatic. They may have happened upon a safe diet because it made them feel better if they ate or avoided eating certain foods.

The so-called "brittle diabetic" is extremely difficult to control and requires extra-careful supervision. This individual goes into shock easily when too much insulin is taken and into coma when it is insufficient. Shock is due to a very low glucose content in the blood. Coma is the result of "burning" too much fat because glucose is not being burned properly resulting in acidosis. The body can burn or metabolize a definite number of grams of fat efficiently. Above that amount, the metabolized fat results in the accumulation of ketones, causing acidosis and coma.

The symptoms of low blood sugar are sweating, anxiety, tremulousness, hunger, and finally shock. A piece of chocolate or sugar, a glass of orange juice, or any sugared beverage will give immediate relief if taken soon enough.

Coma is often ushered in by general malaise, weakness, fatigue, and hyperventilation. It can be a very serious problem, and requires expert hospital and medical care. Hypoglycemic shock can come on very rapidly and is easily treated. Coma usually requires days to develop.

The amount of glucose in the blood of a normal person is astonishingly small—6 to 8 grams (1½ to 2 teaspoonfuls of sugar). As noted, insulin is the hormone required for proper carbohydrate utilization. When glucose rises in the blood through the ingestion of food (this occurs very rapidly from the stomach and small intestines, very often in a matter of minutes), the pancreas reacts by pouring insulin into the bloodstream so that the glucose can be burned in the various tissues or converted into fat or other body constituents. In the diabetic, the blood sugar level rises because it is not being metabolized properly.

The average carbohydrate intake is 300 grams in 24 hours. Remember that two teaspoons of sugar, 2 grams, in a cup of coffee or tea, equals the total amount of glucose circulating in the blood. How then should a diabetic handle his diet? My patients are told to eat the diet that pleases them, avoiding pure sugar and also foods and beverages that have a high sugar content. They should limit their intake of such high carbohydrate foods as the following:

- Cakes, cake mixes, cookies, pie, and rich pastries.
- Candy, chocolate, marshmallows, and other sweets, chewing gum (except sugarless).
- Gelatin desserts, commercial puddings, and other sweetened desserts which contain sugar.
- Jams, jellies, marmalade, preserves.
- Soft drinks, instant cocoa mixes, and other sweetened beverages. Condensed milk.
- Sugar, honey, molasses.

A good many mild diabetics can be controlled simply by diet—that is, their blood sugar can be kept at a fairly normal level below the renal threshold, and sugar will not show in the urine. Diabetic patients are shown how to test their urine with a test tape that will also indicate whether there are ketones present.

If a patient spills sugar while following a sensible diet, one of the oral antidiabetic drugs is employed for treatment. When the condition cannot be controlled by oral antidiabetics, a patient is taught how to use injectable insulin.

The important point here is that generally no complicated diet is necessary. Patients are taught by their doctors how to use their medication in relation to a sensible diet of their liking. They will learn how to handle occasional indiscretions and how various sports and activities will alter medication requirements. An intelligent, informed patient is always a great help to the physician.

The loss of sugar in the urine may cause weight loss and unusual thirst. Weight loss occurs because there is a loss of calories, and thirst because there is an accompanying diuresis and dehydration. Infection will invariably require closer supervision of diet and medication.

I cannot resist a comment on the glucose tolerance test. This is a procedure too frequently used to identify the very mild diabetic. I have occasionally used it when a patient or a physician has insisted. Practically, it has a very very limited value. In this test, the patient is given a measured amount of sugar to drink, and then the blood sugar and urine are tested every half-hour for two to three hours. A routine physical examination which includes the usual laboratory tests will easily identify both the mild and severe diabetic.

Where there is disordered lipid metabolism, proper diet, and drugs, when necessary, can be used to modify and help the condition. Disordered lipid metabolism may be inherited, or may result from poor eating habits. Drug therapy should not be instituted unless diet is ineffective. (See material on cholesterol and lipids in section later on Arteriosclerosis.)

Hypertension (High Blood Pressure)

There are several causes for high blood pressure which are amenable to surgery—a condition called *pheochromocytoma,* and another called *coarctation of the aorta.* Very rarely, occlusion of a renal artery will cause hypertension and require surgery.

Most other causes for high blood pressure are not very well understood and are grouped into a heading, "Essential Hypertension." When the term "essential" is used in medicine, it usually means we don't know the etiology, that is, cause.

Fortunately, there are now a great many effective drugs available for the treatment of hypertension. It is extremely rare not to be able to find an effective combination. In diet, the only important element is the *sodium ion of salt*. Salt should never be added at the table. Foods with a high salt content should be avoided entirely. Obese individuals must maintain an ideal weight. (See listings of "sodium-restricted foods" in section on Congestive Heart Failure.)

Before the advent of successful drug therapy, rice diets were popular and often effective. For those rare individuals who object to taking medications, I have included a typical rice diet. Since the drugs available are so effective, however, I would strongly discourage the use of a rice diet. In either case, proceed under your doctor's supervision.

TYPICAL RICE DIET

Foods to Avoid:

All types of protein food, fats, all types of carbohydrates except those allowed; salt, spices, and all vegetables.

Foods Allowed:

RICE: Rice and rice products . . . rice flakes, boiled rice, puffed rice.

FRUIT: All kinds . . . fresh, canned, frozen, *except* dates and avocado.

SUGAR: White or brown sugar, honey.

FRUIT JUICES: All kinds . . . fresh or canned; no tomato juice, limited to about 1½ pints daily.

SAMPLE DAY'S MENU:

Breakfast:

  8 ounces fruit juice with sugar (2 teaspoons)
  Rice, ½ cup—2 teaspoons sugar
  2 servings fruit
  4 teaspoons jelly

Lunch:

  Rice—½ cup
  2 servings fruit
  8 ounces fruit juice with sugar (2 teaspoons)
  4 teaspoons jelly

Dinner:

  Rice—½ cup
  2 servings fruit
  8 ounces fruit juice with sugar (2 teaspoons)
  4 teaspoons jelly

Arteriosclerosis, Cholesterol and Triglycerides

Arteriosclerosis is defined commonly as "an arterial disease characterized by hardening and thickening of the vessel walls, with lessened blood flow." It occurs predominantly in males after the age of forty, but evidence from postmortem examination of war casualities has revealed that young people may show early evidence of this disease.

Hypertension, diabetes, an inherited disorder of lipid metabolism, and poor eating habits are the most common causes. (Note material in this chapter on Hypertesion and Diabetes.)

Cholesterol and triglycerides have in recent years become familiar terms. Medical experts disagree on which of the two is the more important in the development of arteriosclerosis. International studies of various populations have confirmed that diet will influence the blood level of cholesterol and triglycerides.

The diagnosis and treatment of what is called hyperlipoproteinemia are extremely complex and require expert professional attention. The purpose of this short description is to make available to you in a very simple manner the foods one should consume, and those to avoid, to lower the blood cholesterol and triglycerides. Several drugs are available when diet alone is ineffective.

The basic Scarsdale Medical Diet is low fat and consequently low cholesterol. It is also relatively low in triglyceride-producing foods. It is important in all lipoprotein disorders that obese individuals attain and maintain an ideal weight. The Scarsdale Medical Diet can be a great help. Obviously, your doctor will be monitoring your progress.

THE FOLLOWING HIGH-CHOLESTEROL FOODS SHOULD BE AVOIDED AS MUCH AS POSSIBLE

FATS, OILS, SHORTENINGS—butter, bacon fat, meat fat, poultry fat, lard; saturated (hydrogenated) oils such as coconut oil, olive oil, palm kernel oil; solid shortenings.

DAIRY PRODUCTS—whole milk and whole milk products, cream, sour cream; cheeses made with cream or whole milk; products made with coconut or palm kernel oils or saturated fats (check ingredients on labels).

MEATS—fatty cuts of all meats (always remove visible fat from all meats), bacon, salt pork, spareribs; organ meats, liver, kidneys, brains, sweetbreads; fatty frankfurters, smoked meats, sausages, luncheon meats.

POULTRY—duck, goose. Always remove skin and visible fat from chicken and turkey.

SHELLFISH—avoid overlarge consumption.

EGGS—limit intake to three large eggs a week; unlimited egg whites permitted.

VEGETABLES—avoid avocados; all others permitted.

BREADS, CAKES, DESSERTS, SWEETS—baked goods made with butter, fats, fresh or dried whole eggs such as butter rolls, sweet rolls, doughnuts, high-shortening crackers; cakes, pastries, pies, cookies; rich puddings, ice cream, milk chocolate items.

MISCELLANEOUS—avoid foods fried in butter and saturated fats, creamed foods; canned, frozen, and packaged foods made with butter, shortenings, or other saturated fats.

Where fats and oils are used, they should be *polyunsaturated,* such as corn oil, cottonseed oil, safflower oil, sesame oil, soybean oil, sunflower seed oil, and margarine. Fats and oils are *all* (polyunsaturated, as well as others) high in calories—that's why they are *not* used in the various Scarsdale Diets.

The liver converts carbohydrates to triglycerides. To lower the blood triglycerides, one must avoid the foods noted in the preceding listing, *plus the following high-carbohydrate foods:*

- Cakes, cake mixes, cookies, pie, rich pastries
- Candy, chocolate, marshmallows, other sweets, chewing gum
- Gelatin desserts, commercial puddings, other sweetened desserts which contain sugar
- Jams, jellies, marmalade, preserves
- Soft drinks, instant cocoa mixes, and other sweetened beverages containing sugar; condensed milk
- Sugar, honey, molasses

I must emphasize that people who have hyperlipoproteinemia should be under the careful supervision of a physician. Very often drugs may be necessary to supplement the dietary regime.

These two sentences sum up the basic dietary cautions for patients:

1. Avoid HIGH-FAT foods to help control CHOLESTEROL.

2. Avoid HIGH-CARBOHYDRATE foods to help control TRIGLYCERIDES.

Peptic Ulcer (Stomach—Duodenum)

Frequently *worry* is a contributing factor to peptic ulcer. For that there are no dietary aids. No one can handle your personal problems except you.

As a doctor, I see innumerable tragedies. As a result, I encourage everyone to make the most of each day. Good health is such a magnificent gift, the ability to wake up in the morning, take care of oneself, do new things, see new people, enjoy the well-loved familiar ones—they make me too grateful to worry about most other things.

I like to divide my problems into "good ones" and "bad ones." If you think about it philosophically, many of our everyday problems are "good ones."

Even the exhaustion and aggravations of a very busy day are "good" problems to a large degree. They are often signs of a productive, useful, interesting life, whether it is a hectic day at the office, or a day at home with active, noisy, healthy children.

Usually the things we worry about are not as bad as the illness we create.

The diagnosis of peptic ulcer is usually extremely simple, since the symptoms are so characteristic—upper, mid-abdominal pain generally coming on about one hour after eating. Pain frequently awakens the patient during the night, and is often accompanied by upper, mid-abdominal tenderness. Abdominal discomfort is relieved by antacids or eating.

Symptoms are usually aggravated by coffee, alcohol, and spices.

A "therapeutic test" is frequently more valuable than an X-ray GI series, since only 70 percent of ulcers can be visualized. In practice, I prefer to treat rather than X-ray for diagnosis.

ULCER DIET

Foods to Avoid:

- Coffee and tea
- All fatty and fried foods, including gravies
- Smoked and preserved meats and fish
- Pork
- Spices and condiments
- Meat soups
- Tomatoes, tomato juice, tomato soup
- Pastries, preserves, nuts, candies
- Stimulants and carbonated waters
- Alcohol

Antacids are taken between meals and before retiring. They are also employed for relief of pain and discomfort at any time.

A great many drugs are also available—some of the newer ones are particularly effective. Consult your doctor.

It usually takes about six weeks to cure an ulcer, although the symptoms are relieved in a few days. Ulcers are often recurrent, especially in the spring and fall. *An old ulcer* with fibrotic borders and base may be resistant to therapy.

The diet treatment for *hiatus hernia* and *esophagitis* is similar to that of peptic ulcer.

Heartburn, Indigestion

This is the third most common intestinal complaint. It is extremely unpleasant and uncomfortable, but, as your doctor will agree, rarely, if ever, a serious condition. The discomfort is usually described as a burning sensation vaguely located behind the middle of the chest.

The most frequent cause is coffee, and foods preserved in sodium benzoate. Oddly, fresh oranges and juice are well tolerated, while other orange preparations are not. Spices, fried foods, chocolate, onions, and cucumbers, are other foods which may initiate this symptom.

Each individual must review the food eaten one-half to two hours previous to onset of the symptoms, to determine what he cannot tolerate—then avoid the offending foods, or limit intake.

Personally, I have found that when I am under a great deal of stress, I am more apt to have this problem. Remember to help yourself by determining whether you have a "good" or "bad" problem.

There are innumerable antacids available for relief. It is best to try a number, and use the one that has the most agreeable taste, and gives complete relief. There is absolutely no need to suffer this discomfort longer than it takes to down an antacid.

Because it is easy to obtain complete relief, most people are willing to put up with the discomfort rather than forego a food or beverage they like. Obviously, an individual choice.

Gall Bladder Disease

A gall bladder without stones rarely causes the typical symptoms of gall bladder disease—indigestion, feeling of fullness, belching, flatulence, and/or pain. Acute upper abdominal pain, usually severe, with tenderness in the right upper or mid-abdomen, is almost diagnostic. The pain frequently radiates to the right shoulder blade.

The symptoms usually occur a couple of hours after a heavy meal, very often in the middle of the night. The urine is frequently dark and the stools light, because bile is not entering the small bowel.

Most surgeons insist on surgical removal of a gall bladder containing stones; I must say that with modern surgery and its excellent results, they are justified. In the elderly, however, I usually advise my patients to have surgery only if they are having symptoms that cannot be controlled by avoiding fried foods and foods high in fat.

A few research centers are experimenting with a substance that will dissolve gall stones, but at this time we have no sure way of removing them short of surgery.

BASIC DIET PROCEDURES

DAIRY FOODS: NO whole milk or cream. Permitted —skim milk, fat-free buttermilk, skim-evaporated milk. NO CHEESE other than low-fat pot cheese, low-fat cottage cheese, ricotta.

MEATS, POULTRY: NO pork and pork products, duck and goose. Permitted—lean meats, chicken, turkey—all visible fat and skin removed before eating.

FISH: NO fat fish such as mackerel, herring, lox. Permitted—lean fish such as bass, bluefish, cod, flounder, haddock, perch, whitefish; shellfish—fresh, frozen, and canned without oil.

VEGETABLES: Vegetables which agree with you are permitted—raw, cooked, canned, frozen.

FRUITS: Fruits and fruit juices which agree with you are permitted, without skins or seeds.

EGGS: Only ONE egg daily if tolerated—boiled, poached, coddled, but not fried. Egg whites permitted as wanted.

BREADS, CEREALS: NO hot breads, biscuits, waffles, muffins.

DESSERTS: NO pastries, pies, chocolate, ice cream; no desserts made with butter, shortening, margarine, whole milk. Permitted—skim milk desserts, other desserts made with egg white, such as angel food cake, meringues, vanilla macaroons.

SOUPS: NO cream soups; meat, or chicken soups from which fat has not been removed. Permitted— bouillon, broth, consommé; meat, poultry, fish soups with fat removed; vegetable soups made with vegetables that agree with you.

FATS: NO fats such as sweet and sour cream, salad oil, vegetable shortenings, lard, mayonnaise. Permitted —a maximum of three teaspoons daily of butter or margarine, if tolerated.

SEASONINGS: Salt, pepper, spices, herbs may be used in moderation.

SUGAR, jelly, syrup, honey permitted in moderation.

NO NUTS, peanut butter, olives.

NO MEAT GRAVIES, meat sauces, cream sauces, "white" sauces.

Constipation

Today's hectic pace leaves insufficient time for a proper bowel movement. The intestine literally has to scream for attention to this vital function.

It is extremely important for the individual to develop a bowel routine—try to leave time after breakfast. With a sincere effort, most people are able to establish a conditioned reflex.

Prunes, prune juice, various compotes, bulk cereals, and a host of so-called "roughage items" can be found to suit the individual's tastes and needs. *Senna and licorice products* have been taken with impunity and great satisfaction for many decades—they are easily varied to one's needs. A cathartic should never be taken in the presence of nausea, vomiting, or abdominal pain. If there is real discomfort, see your doctor.

The following basic roughage-diet information may be helpful:

HIGH-FIBER, HIGH-BULK EATING GUIDELINES

High-fiber, high-bulk foods help the "mechanics of digestion," thus combat constipation by promoting elimination of waste materials. Basically, a diet containing high-fiber roughage foods would include:

FRUITS—preferably eaten raw (with skins and seeds, where possible); dried fruits, prunes, prune juice.

VEGETABLES—preferably eaten raw, or with a minimum of cooking.

SALADS—plenty of mixed greens, lettuce, carrots, celery, cucumbers, tomatoes, raw spinach, broccoli, cauliflower.

CEREALS—all-bran and whole-grain types especially, dry and cooked, have highest fiber content; most dry cereals (preferably without sugar) have sizable fiber content.

BREADS—whole-grain and bran breads have higher fiber content; refined white breads have very little fiber.

IMPORTANT—drink large quantities of WATER, 8 to 10 glasses daily, especially at meals, for best effect. Fiber swells as it absorbs water, adds more bulk.

While high-fiber, high-bulk foods are effective in helping to control constipation, it must be emphasized that "fiber" in foods is just one element. It's not "magic," not a panacea, and certainly not a great reducing aid for overweights since fiber foods such as cereals and breads are relatively high in calories. Therefore, high-fiber foods must be eaten in moderation, observing these general guidelines:

• Include moderate amounts of low-fat meats, poultry, fish, for protein and other elements.

• Avoid sweets, rich desserts, cakes, pastries, sugar and starch foods—practically all are low in fiber and high in calories.

• Eggs, milk, cheese have their own values but little or no fiber.

Common sense is an all-important guide in high-fiber roughage eating. Effects vary with each individual. It makes sense to add high-fiber bulk to the diet when needed for regular bowel movements. Then it's up to the person to add or reduce roughage consumption as needed. Checking with your personal physician is essential if you have a change in bowel habits.

INDEX

213

N

ABOUT THE AUTHORS

HERMAN TARNOWER, M.D., FACP, D-IM (cv), distinguished cardiologist and internist, was founder and
senior member of the Scarsdale, New York, Medical
Center; honorary president and chairman of the board
of Westchester Heart Association. Before his death in
1980, he was clinical professor of medicine, New York
Medical College; attending cardiologist, White Plains
Hospital; consulting cardiologist, St. Agnes Hospital,
White Plains, New York.

SAMM SINCLAIR BAKER, described in *The New York
Times* as "America's leading self-help author," has
written twenty-six books, including some notable best-
sellers.